Close Your Back Door

As You

Widen the Front Door

Of

Your Church

A Practical Approach to Church Development and Empowerment

Leonard Lovett

Close Your Back Door as You Widen the Front Door of Your Church
by Leonard Lovett

Copyright © 1998 Leonard Lovett. All rights reserved. No part of this book may be reproduced in any form without permission in writing from the author or publisher, except in the case of brief quotations embodied in church related publications, critical articles or reviews. Write to: Morris Publishing 3212 East Highway 30 . Kearney, NE 68847. 1-800-650-7888

All Scripture quotations, unless noted otherwise, are from the Holy Bible, New International Version, Copyright © 1973, 1978, 1984 International Bible Society. Used by permission of Zondervan Bible Publishers.

Quotations from the King James Version have been denoted (KJV).

Printed in the United States of America

Copyright 1998
Leonard Lovett Ph.D
ISBN: 1-57502-874-3
Library of Congress Catalog Card Number: 98-91607

Printed in the USA by
MORRIS PUBLISHING
3212 East Hwy. 30
Kearney, NE 68847
1-800-650-7888

Dedicated to the Chief Servants of the Church of God In Christ
(1996 - 2000)

Bishop Chandler David Owens *Presiding Bishop*

Bishop J. Neaul Haynes *First Assistant Presiding Bishop*

Bishop Ozro Thurston Jones, Jr. *Second Presiding Bishop*

Bishop Cleveland L. Anderson, Jr. *Assistant Presiding Bishop Emeritus*

Bishop Phillip A. Brooks *General Board Secretary*

Bishop Samuel L. Green *Assistant General Board Secretary*

Bishop Roy L.H. Winbush

Bishop Charles E. Blake

Bishop Gilbert E. Patterson

Bishop Ithiel C. Clemmons

Bishop Leroy R. Anderson

Bishop Levi L. Willis

Bishop W.W. Hamilton *General Secretary*

Mother Willie M. Rivers *General Supervisor*

CONTENTS iii

ACKNOWLEDGMENTS

INTRODUCTORY PREFACE

Part I

Widen the Front Door of Your Church: On Expansion

Chapter 1 *What My Mentors Missed*
An Idea is Born ● Why Networking Pays Off ● Positive Attitudes Work ● If You Focus On Quality......Quantity Will Come

Chapter 2 *Monitor Your Front Door*
Answer Only Seven.........Questions ● When Front Door Gains and Back Door Loss Equals Same Size ● Maximize Your Potential ● Why Not Brighten the Corners.....Within Your Community ● Avoid Placing Dreams On Hold

Chapter 3 **Making the Front Door the Right Door**
A Winning Combination: Word and Deed ● Revival and Evangelism: Similar But Different ● Why Dynamic Worship is Magnetic ● Be Open to Change

Chapter 4 *This Key Works...The Master Speaks*
Expanding His Kingdom in the World ● Cultivating the Marriage Between Pastor and People ● When the Death of A Church Means Life ● When Nibbles Becomes Bites.....Only in Fishing

Chapter 5 *Liberate and Reclaim Your City*
Sources of Inner City Misery ● Urban Challenges....Demons With a New Address ● Political Primacy....Achieving the Possible ● The Church is......What It Does

PART II
Close Your Back Door: On Retention

Chapter 6 *Revolving Doors: A Challenge For Churches*
The Problem That Will Not Leave ● Red Flags, Red Herrings and Back Door Loss ● Using Failure To Your Advantage ● Members Must Be Free To Leave

Chapter 7 *Bolting All Side Doors: Handling Small Things*
Let's Park Our Automobile ● Why Security is Important ● How Does Your Community View Your Church? ● Does Information Flow Through Your Church?

Chapter 8 *From the Inside Out: Evaluating Five Key Areas*
Urban Ministry Outreach: Reaching the Lost At Whatever Cost ● Worship and Music Inventory: Let's Dance ● Christian Nurture and Counseling Inventory: Does Anyone Care? ● Youth Inventory: What's Up Doc? ● Stewardship Inventory: God Does Not Want Your Money

Chapter 9 *Discovery: Its the Best Lock*
Why Bother Joining A Church? ● Should New Member Orientation Be Optional? ● Indoctrination or Discipleship?......Which Shall It Be? ● The Adoption Plan: Transitioning To a New Environment ● Communion With God: Just Keep On Praying ● Communicating with Others: Keep On Talking

Chapter 10 *Passion: Close Your Back Door Permanently*
Let's Try Scratching Where People Are Itching ● Developing and Cultivating Interpersonal Relationships ● Its Way Pastime to Free the Sisters ● Create A Place For Men ● Mobilization: Unleashing Our Potential ● Unity: We Are In This Together

EPILOGUE   *Kingdom Hope and Possibilities for the City*
APPENDIX
SOURCE NOTES
BIBLIOGRAPHY

ACKNOWLEDGMENTS

Seldom does one find a book of any substance written without considerable influence from a variety of individuals, experiences and forces that have impacted the author's life. It is not modest to confess that we are all products of our environment, but more significantly our thoughts and experiences are dramatically impacted by a collectivity of persons we encounter on our life's pilgrimage. Such has been the case with me. I too stand on the shoulders of many persons. My writing like every author, is a blend of life experiences, formal education, and generous, godly and wise individuals who have been at the proper stations at the right time of my journey.

My gratitude is extended to the many pastors, lay leaders, faculty colleagues, and students who have provided invaluable insight on how to expand and share my ministry ideas more effectively. They are far too numerous to mention. They will appear in nerve and fiber of what I have written as adequate testimony that they are striving to be the best they can be for God. To these "Angels of the Churches" I extend my deepest gratitude.

This work was not conceived in isolation within the ivory towers of academia, but from the corpus of a live church experience in the heart of Philadelphia, Atlanta and Los Angeles. It was conceived in the cauldron of trial and failure. The Incarnation has to be realized within the "blood and guts" of our daily strivings. The insights gleaned in this book grew as I have conducted scores of seminars with small to medium churches in North America and Canada. It is the result of open honest dialogue from a pastor to pastors from storefronts to cathedrals as I have criss-crossed this nation by plane, train, bus and automobile. Finally I express my deepest gratitude to God who has promised His presence to the end of the age.

INTRODUCTORY PREFACE

If you are searching for a "three steps to rescuing your church" manual, you have selected the wrong book. Do yourself a favor by correctly placing the book in its rightful place on the shelf. My ministry to the Body of Christ is similar and comparable to that of an internist in medicine. I am committed to finding the source of the problem and think biblically and theologically in a prescriptive way about resolving same. However, I believe with conviction that this book will in time become the rightful property of only those persons in search of a creative and practical approach to the perennial problem of membership retention for churches in an urban environment largely characterized by consumerism.

The statistics are in from the experts. Our world is increasingly becoming urbanized. From India's coral strand to the far reaches of South America, from the most isolated region of the vast continent of Africa to the far reaches of Asia and on to the smallest hamlets of Europe, the facts are similar. Our technology has brought us together. We must begin to think globally and act locally in an urbanized world!

The major thrust of this book is to broadened the perspective of the church leader who wants to develop and maintain a productive ministry within a relational church. **Part I** deals with *expansion* and qualitative growth of one's ministry. You will find insights from my previous book, <u>**OPENING THE FRONT DOOR OF YOUR CHURCH**</u> embodied and reinterpreted within this work. What I discussed four years ago is foundational to my present discussion. The conversation and discussion has grown with a different group of participants at the round table. My discussion continues to be dialogue simply because I do not believe no one has "said it all." To mature is to learn from the insight and wisdom garnered from others. I am a student in the school of life.

The environment in which the church must make its witness has been impacted by a form of secularism unknown to modern humankind. The social prognosis for the pathology within the African-American community is shocking. Two and a half years of double-digit inflation has already disarmed many Blacks for the beginning millennia. Everything that isn't nailed down is coming up. We are experiencing the "shaking of the

Introductory preface

foundations" to borrow a Tillichean phrase. Hot house growth is no longer tenable for the Christian church if it is to survive in today's environment. Reaching Generation Xers (In algebraic equations X is the symbol for unknown quantity), requires a far different method than that of their parents "Baby Busters and Boomers." The generational values and lifestyle are vast distances apart.

Our strategies must never be merely cosmetic but should always have Cosmic backing. Our spiritual roots must be deeper, our faith assured and our methods for ministry must indeed reflect the mandates of the Kingdom. Our emphasis must shift to "what kind" rather then" how many." It is not less than growth, but much more than growth for quantity sakes.

The Front Door of your church can now be widened in creative ways, employing effective strategies that reflect a new shift in models. Many models of the past that were effective need to be maintained. Other models must be abandoned because they are irrelevant to the variety of ways and expressions of God's actions in the contemporary environment. God is "doing a new thing." Most pastors in some way struggle with this continuing concern. The good news is that there are creative ways to minimize losses and assist your congregation in their growth toward maturity. New members can be effectively assimilated into your church.

Whether it is biological transfer or conversion growth, you can effectively widen the front door of your church in creative ways that are productive. Bishop T.D. Jakes, popular African-American Evangelist-Pastor, recently transitioned his ministry from West Virginia to the Dallas - Ft. Worth area and opened the Potters House. Within two years according to some reports there are some 5,000 plus in attendance. Much of the growth taking place at the Potters House is transfer growth and not conversion. In transfer growth, the challenges will be greater in assimilating new people due to the variety and confluence of religious agendas. Unless a serious discipling process is in place, Jakes could grow an anemic church. There are still many unchurched people in North America. Alas, the ends of the earth have come to North America. In most of our urban areas, we can discover a microcosm of the international community. This means that we must be willing to undergo a paradigm shift if we are to truly lead the lost to Jesus Christ.

Part II deals with *retention*. Closing the backdoor of the church is no easy and simple matter. I deliberately entered the trenches with the "grease and grime" problems and situations the church must face sooner or later in urbia if it is to maintain a credible witness.

Needless to say we have become prisoners against our will within our own houses due to the proliferation of high crime, our cities have become urban war zones, largely by gang and ethnic turf battles. Add to this drug and substance abuse in the midst of eroding infrastructures, it is easy to conclude that we are living a nightmare. Our problems are so pronounced, no political party can resolve them with "quick fix" solutions. That is why the very values we often espouse and embrace in our times must be challenged and critiqued by Scripture and the radical mandates of the Kingdom. The real task of ministry begins once the "front door" of your church begins to widen. The emphasis must be directed toward those newcomers to the fold who indeed ought to be embraced with a 'love that will not let them go.' It may very well mean revamping the way we used to do things and re-gearing for persons whose minds have been shaped and impacted by modernity. Today's church ought never be conceived of as a prison where members are indirectly and directly pressured against their will.

Once the church loses its voluntary character, it is no longer the Church of Jesus Christ. Sooner or later most churches must face the "backdoor" and "side door" problem of losing members. For the most part we live in a mobile society. We are invariably influenced by the status symbols of upward mobility and class. Modern mass media does shape much of our value system. The reality that people come and go is a fact of life in modern society. However, when they leave the church, it is crucial to ascertain precisely why persons exit our ministry, often without any warning or prior notice, if we really care.

The good news is that you can "close" the backdoor of your church without giving members the feeling that they are on a tight ship suffocating for air because of stringent, inflexible, and sometimes "dictatorial" hard fast rules designed to keep the troops in line. Not only can you "close" the backdoor of your church, but you can place a permanent lock on it. Since "backdoor" loss is a perennial challenge that will not just evaporate, but in fact can be minimized, you will learn how to use failure to your advantage.

There is growing empirical data to support the reasons why some churches are able to retain members in contrast to others. Something dynamic is taking place within key ministry areas within these churches that provides a deep sense of security and well-being to believers who really want to follow their Lord through His church. When was the last time you seriously "inventoried" your ministry from the inside out?

What is really going on with Evangelism Outreach...does it have an urban twist? Will diverse people groups within the urban icon be impacted by your message? What about Music and Worship....is it relational and meaningful? What about Youth Ministry and Christian Nurture...do they find the hearts for whom they were intended? What about Stewardship....are members pressured to give by shrewd psychological overt tactics? Even the United States Congress has a check and balance system, designed to encourage accountability.

Why do churches who *make membership important* grow and retain members in greater contrast to churches who use a matter-of-fact attitude toward their membership? Is *new member orientation* a necessity ? Why do churches who insist on *new member orientation* invariably minimize their attrition rate and develop a different genre of members than those who do not?

When new members can find their place in a church without a great deal of stress and strain, they usually end up feeling at home. In the words of Dr. James Dobson, child psychologist, *home is where the heart is.* Once members are assimilated within a new church environment, they need support systems. Developing a new member adoption system provides a necessary link to staying in touch with new members through the ministry of caring. Once systematic *discipleship* is utilized rather than indoctrination , you are ready to permanently *lock the backdoor of your church..* The People of God must be given a sense of ownership as they walk in the dignity conferred upon them by the Sinless One.

This book is specific, deliberate and intentional because it attempts to address a concern that comes up in pastoral settings and conferences. To what extent must pastors hone their managerial skills in ministry? Some pastors are comfortable as visionaries but cannot handle simple managerial tasks. Some pastors are at home with preaching tasks but come up short in interpersonal relations. I trust that this book will simplify and challenge such leadership potential as you shepherd God's people.

This book is also intended to provide options for pastors who are perennially frustrated by the challenge of people in transition. The hope is that a "new" perspective will be provided that will enable pastoral leaders to approach an old problem from the standpoint of advantage. Practical insights found in this work are not exclusively my own. They come from many places, persons, experiences, failures, faltering aspirations and hope. However I take responsibility for the final form in which these ideas are presented.

Ours is a world of rapid societal changes that often impact the way we think about problems and engage in the momentous task of problem-solving.

This book is also written from the perspective of one who has been grasped by the mandates of the Kingdom of God. There is no substitute for experience. Several years ago would have produced a different kind of book. My theology has been impacted by my perspective of the Kingdom. Once the "red flags" of back door loss occur we must skillfully rise to address the situation, armed with a winning perspective. To do anything less would be counter-productive to the mandates of the Kingdom.

Using the metaphor of a door I have endeavored to share my heart in order to enable you to close the back door of your church. Since my last book I simply "tweaked" the metaphor. Most doors are already open. Some doors are barely cracked open. Others are partially open. Yes I am guilty! After four years in the Washington metro area and some 125 seminars later, I realized something about most churches. Those doors can be opened a little wider. I am like the person looking for their eye glasses, only to discover that they are wearing them! I radically challenge you to focus and become intentional about "closing the backdoor" of your church as you "widen the Front Door."

Fasten your seat belt and relax as we journey by faith to special places, develop creative approaches and myriad ways of maximizing the effectiveness of your church. The impetus to embark upon such a journey is grounded in Scripture. (Daniel 12:3) *And they that be wise shall shine as the brightness of the firmament; and they that turn many to righteousness as the stars for ever and ever.* Bon Voyage!

chapter
1
What My Mentors Missed

An Idea is Born

I arrived at Morehouse College the same month Dr. Martin Luther King, Jr. returned to launch a serious campaign against segregation, a formidable foe during those days. I observed robed Klansman on one side of the street as we struggled against injustice in the market place. I majored in history with a minor in religion and social science during my undergraduate studies. While interesting and challenging I knew there was much more. I was introduced to the Niebuhr brothers, Reinhold and H. Richard, Paul Tillich, Martin Buber, Dietrich Bonhoeffer and the list goes on. I first heard the late Dr. Vernon Johns, Mordecai Johnson, Howard Thurman and many other prominent African-American theologians, preachers and scholars brought to Morehouse by the late eminent educator and scholar, Dr. Benjamin Mays. I intuitively knew then there was more. Dr. Samuel Williams, Melvin Watson, Murray Branch, and Lucius Tobin provided the finest philosophical and theological challenges of any major educational institution in North America, and yet there was more.

My classical seminary education began at Crozer Theological Seminary which was located in Chester, Pennsylvania at that time. My seminary training began two years after President John F. Kennedy launched the New Frontier and was completed just as President Lyndon Baines Johnson was launching his Great Society program targeting the elimination of rampant poverty as one of its primary goals.

A new kind of optimism overshadowed our nation as we slowly became involved in Vietnam. By then I had become bi-vocational while I worked on a degree in community organization at Bryn Mawr Graduate School of Social

Research and took on my first pastoral assignment in Haverford, Pennsylvania at Memorial Church of God in Christ. With the launching of President Lyndon Baines Johnson's Great Society, I was caught between the idealism of my seminary professors and the realism of how to functionally administer my first pastorate as a novice. Even then my bright, brash and challenging professors did not provide clear cut answers to the inner city problems of Philadelphia that I encountered during my first job in the public sector. I walked the streets of Philadelphia as a Neighborhood Youth Corps Coordinator looking for at risk youth who had dropped out of school for myriad reasons.

More than a century ago, Charles Dickens poignantly described the spirit that characterized the decades of the sixties and the seventies as he wrote: "It was the best of times; it was the worst of times. It was the age of wisdom; it was the age of foolishness . It was the epoch of belief; it was the epoch of incredulity... It was the spring of hope it was the winter of despair. We had everything before us; we had nothing before us."

Any minimal success achieved during those times must be attributed to excellent mentors such as Bishop O. T. Jones, Jr. jurisdictional Bishop of the Commonwealth of Pennsylvania and Second Assistant Presiding Bishop of the Churches of God in Christ who had preceded me as pastor. I suggest that all pastors find someone to whom they can be responsible as a mentor and for the sake of accountability. You will face issues in ministry that only an experienced person can weave their way through. Many experienced leaders have already been where you are planning to go. There is a Paul for every Timothy in ministry. Take care of this matter at once. As a new pastor I was off to a good start because I utilized the counsel of pastors who had an excellent track record.

My first assignment was to revitalize the total teaching ministries of that local parish beginning with Sunday School. Motivated by the urge to practice and implement what I had learned in Seminary, I spent time gathering data. Ironically, that was where my first real education began. During a seven year pastorate, the church responded to my leadership. As a medium congregation we never exceeded two hundred and fifty in membership, but came to occupy a place of prominence and influence in that suburban Philadelphia community.

During the summer of 1970, I responded to my denomination's call to pioneer the first fully accredited Pentecostal Seminary in North America, the Charles H. Mason Theological Seminary, an affiliate of the Interdenominational Theological Center, Atlanta, Georgia. After four challenging years I tendered my resignation in order to devote full time to the completion of my doctoral studies at Emory University.

During the summer of 1976, I was appointed to the Church at the Crossroads Peniel Church of God In Christ, located in the heart of South Central Los Angeles by the late Bishop Samuel Crouch against all odds of surviving. Eleven years prior to my new assignment, one of the worst civil disturbances in modern urban history, the Watts riot, had virtually devastated the neighboring community. Upon arrival I discovered that I was in the midst of a congregation that had been severed by an intergenerational ideological split. The Bishop's appointment of yours truly was indeed controversial.

While en route from Atlanta, I learned that the church had been torched by an unknown arsonist. Upon my arrival for the first worship service as Pastor, I was greeted by dissidents who were strongly opposed to the appointment. As I look back, only the Holy Spirit enabled me to remain focused as we praised God in the midst of the worst of times.

During the ensuing months, we initiated the church's first unified budget system, staff organization and total reorganization of the Church and expanded the name by adding Crossroads. We learned from that experience that timing can make or break a church in transition. Sometimes the new idea is great, but it is simply not the time to implement it. Relationships must always set the stage for programmatic changes. People tend to be more open to acceptance of new ideas once trust has been established. An effectual door of opportunity had been opened to me, but there were many adversaries (1 Corinthians 16:9). The desire to expand came to fruition after the third year as pastoral leader. I had earned the right to be called Pastor. I encountered experiences no seminary could adequately prepare one to serve. The experience of serving as a local church pastor continues the education that began in seminary.[1]

WHY NETWORKING PAYS OFF

During the Fall of 77, I had accepted a position at Fuller Theological Seminary, Pasadena, California, home of the celebrated New Year Rose bowl Parade. I served as Associate Director of Black Ministries to Dr. William Pannell for several years. I also taught in my academic field, theological and social ethics. The Black Ministries program exposed me first hand to pastors with serious pastoral concerns and to the Fuller School of World Mission, with its developing and unique church growth emphasis and agenda. I tried to read as much church growth theory as possible with an ear tuned for any related concerns.

From the Fuller experience I discovered that a great deal of modern church growth theory is relative and is not necessarily applicable and related to all churches, particularly many minority ethnic churches. On the other hand, any theory has to be adapted to particular situations, whether it be George Barna, Peter Wagner or Robert Schuller.

In the mid seventies Jerry Macklin and I interfaced for the first time. I recall Jerry and his wife Vanessa starting a mission church from his living room. We shared and exchanged ministry ideas after I took a pastorate in Los Angeles. While traveling different paths we can both attest to the fact that God alone blesses the harvest. Today, as a result of Jerry's persistence and desire for the Kingdom, Glad Tidings Church has to be reckoned with as one of the best organized and leading churches in the Northern California Bay area in our denomination. They have transformed the neighborhood form a drug infested haven to a livable environment. Currently Dr. Macklin is President of (AIM) Auxiliaries in Ministry Convention for the Church of God in Christ. It all started by networking with a friend who wanted to expand his ministry on behalf of God's Kingdom.

Quantity is not decisive when it comes to building a church of influence

The primary issue then that gave birth to the idea of this book was what are the kinds of things that we can do to enable a church to maximize its effectiveness? What goes into the menu? What constitutes the equation? What can we think through that can benefit the seventy-five percent of small to medium churches in North America who may never become a mega-church, but could maximize their effectiveness and constitute churches of influence. Quantity is not decisive when it comes to building a church of influence. It's like the commercial about Zenith, the quality goes in before the name goes on.

A secondary concern that gave birth to this work was to what extent is it possible to shift the focus from mega-trends to peoplehood from developing church people to Kingdom people, from quantitative factors to qualitative issues that bear the sign and mark of the Kingdom. [2] The church must be more than bricks and mortar, it is the bearer of an ancient story that constitutes good news.

What I offer to you then is a perspective that has been honed, refined and nurtured within the context of experience, debate and dialogue. It is not a final solution to growth and retention, nor is it the ultimate panacea. Rather, I am providing you with tried and proven techniques, specialized information about how to discern your vision, analyze your church environment, and ways to implement and develop your ministry. The way this information is utilized and employed will determine the outcome. Remember your angle of vision is crucial. I pray that the information provided will be a first step toward what it means to widen the front door (expansion) and close the back door (retention) of your church. A serious issue facing most churches is expansion and retention. At least ninety-eight percent of the pastors interviewed the past several years admitted that this is one of the most serious issues facing their ministry.

Mutual agreement to expand and a trust relationship are prerequisites for meaningful growth

Mutual agreement to expand is a prerequisite for meaningful growth. For meaningful growth to occur (some growth is premature and usually experiences an untimely demise), both pastor and congregation must mutually desire to grow. A pastor recently admitted, while I would like to grow and expand, my people have become ingrown, comfortable and complacent. If the pastor and his or her congregation are not in agreement on growth, the outcome will be greatly altered. Some pastors are satisfied with merely maintaining the status quo of their present congregations. Similarly, some parishioners are threatened by the possibilities of displacement by newcomers. Smallness is equated with intimacy by many parishioners. From personal experience I can say this need not be the case.

A trust relationship is a prerequisite for solid growth. A relationship of mutual trust between both pastor and congregation must be cultivated and maintained for mutual growth to occur. Certain church growth theorists contend that it takes at least five years for a congregation to develop a meaningful trust relationship with its leaders. In the New Testament, we discover that the early church grew as it came under severe persecution. Persecution from without has a unique way of bonding together leaders and congregation. Thus trust becomes a primary ingredient for meaningful church expansion.

Planning, prayer and work are foundational prerequisites for qualitative growth. The pastor and congregation must plan, pray and work on behalf of qualitative church expansion. Such planning must surely involve a key leadership team and a congregational nucleus ready to invest time, energy and resources on behalf of the kingdom. A workable plan must accompany the desire to expand. Priority must be given to developing a master plan of strategy and outreach.

Prayer admits us into God's presence for commitment, cleansing and decision making.[3] The pastor who desires to expand must undergird his or her best-laid plans with continuous prayer. While evangelism involves techniques and strategies to win people to Christ, prayer gives vitality and life to the total process. An hour-long prayer service held each Monday evening was the spark for qualitative expansion. A committed nucleus comes together for confession, mutual affirmation and guidance by the Holy Spirit.

Work goes well in the context of planning and prayer. Work on behalf of the kingdom differs from busy church work, which is often ingrown and introverted. Kingdom work involves not only leading persons to Christ and making disciples of all nations, but working on their behalf to create an environment where authentic nurture can take place. Such work must encompass seeking justice and relieving conditions of oppression. Relieving hunger and homelessness are examples of issues that require serious agents of the kingdom who understand that qualitative growth takes place when the soil has been prepared. While the Kingdom ought to be viewed as a "disturbing community", it would be wrong to think of Jesus as a sort of celestial consumer advocate.[4]

POSITIVE ATTITUDES WORK

Attitude at one level of definition means posture position, pose and stand. Our perspective is invariably shaped by our attitude. Whether we will succeed or fail is largely determined by our attitude. Attitude determines whether we will soar with eagles or simply be like prairie chickens. Whether you are an athlete or air traffic controller, a manager or maid, a postal worker or pastor, attitude determines altitude. Charles Swindoll has so eloquently articulated the importance of attitude for the whole of our lives.

"The longer I live, the more I realize the impact of attitude on life. Attitude to me, is more important than facts. It is more important than the past, than education, than money, than circumstances, than failures, than successes, than what other people think or say or do. It is more important than appearance, giftedness, or skill. It will make or break a company...a church...a home. The remarkable thing is we have a

choice everyday regarding the attitude we will embrace for that day. We cannot change our past...we cannot change the fact that people will act in a certain way. We cannot change the inevitable. The only thing we can do is play on the one string we have, and that is our attitude... I am convinced that life is 10% what happens to me and 90% how I react to it. And so it is with you...we are in charge of our attitudes." [5]

Expanding one's ministry must become a part of our dreams and desires. It must dominate our thoughts and saturate the passages of our mind. It means being the best you can be for God on behalf of His Kingdom. It means achieving excellence as we live out the meaning of our witness. Perhaps the poet Douglas Mallock had this in mind when he so graphically wrote:

"If you can't be a pine on the top of the hill be a scrub in the valley-but be the best little scrub by the side of the hill, be a bush, if you can't be a tree. If you can't be a highway, just be a trail. If you can't be a sun, be a star; It isn't by size, that you win or fail... Be the best of whatever you are."

Congregations have personality, that reflects a positive or negative syndrome. Attitudes develop from the congregations corporate personality traits. Mutual agreement to expand as a body of believers entails overcoming negativity and building esteem. When leaders are positive, they impact the congregation in decisive ways. To overcome negative attitudes within a congregation requires thoughtful discernment and wise planning. Once attitudes are identified, a plan to confront them can be developed. Building consensus within a congregation can take place in the midst of negative hindrances within the body if the leader is skillful in managing conflict and can build positive relationships.

Wise leaders surround themselves with individuals who can intercede and build strong interpersonal relationships

The significance of intercessory prayer must be underscored as one of the most effective means of confronting congregational attitudinal difficulties. Wise leaders surround themselves with individuals who can intercede and build strong interpersonal relationships. Prayer ushers us into God's presence for cleansing and decision-making. Develop a core group that will intercede until attitudes are changed, that will be the beginning of a new era for your church.

Set a specific time and insist on punctuality. Be prepared to overcome evil with good. Document the activity, mission and assignment for the core group. Watch for the change in congregational attitudes as the Holy Spirit melts anxious hearts. Faithfulness to God sets the stage for change. Get ready to mount up with wings as eagles, you are now ready for the high places. Allow God to order your steps.

If You Focus On Quality.......Quantity Will Come

William Arthur Ward once said, *"the mediocre teacher tells, the good teacher explains, the superior teacher demonstrates, the great teacher inspires."* Having been exposed to the best, there were gaps and deficiencies in my training. Excellent theory makes good practice, but theory is not practice. My seminary training provided necessary tools for ministry and certain rules for the road but did not equip me for dealing with all kinds of road hazards.

The higher one ascends, the need for proper equipment becomes crucial. The air is much thinner at 70,000 feet than at 20,000. Oxygen is crucial at 70,000 feet. Many congregations remain the same after many years, not because of their church attendance, but due to a misunderstanding of basic human nature. In my life time, I have watched brilliant preachers give up in frustration at a time when everyone thought all was well. I have observed mediocre leaders succeed where prevailing predictions were no more than one year. Human nature has not changed. Ananias and Sapphira now wear designer clothes and have learned how to dress and parade the truth in the garb of modernity.

I learned about Brunner, Barth, Bonhoeffer and Bultmann, but not too much about the "games people play" in the congregational arena

With all due respect to my Seminary Professors both living and deceased, they did not prepare me to deal with "neurotics" in the church who scheme and skillfully plan the demise of the leader, too often for what they perceive to be the right reasons. I learned about Brunner, Barth, Bonhoeffer and Bultmann, but not too much about the "games people play" in the congregational arena. Control is the name of the power game within churches that lead to years of unresolved tensions. How to control either the pulpit or deacon/trustee board directly or indirectly. How organized cliques develop and maintain power bases.

What should one do when a congregation develops a "we shall not be moved attitude.?" Road hazards are often made more dangerous not by the seen, but rather the unseen. It is the surprise pothole, or black ice in the winter, or nails and broken glass that is often invisible until the initial moment of contact that constitutes immediate danger.

There are sociological factors, geographical barriers which invariably influence church activity. The values, customs, habits, traditions of a congregation are crucial to understand in coping with future problems that emerge unexpectedly. In the words of Lloyd Perry, "these are dangerous days for the organized church. It is time to be alert to what is taking place and to make some changes."[6] Many seminaries have already begun the process of providing a more realistic practicum for students while in training. Exposure to experienced pastors can provide invaluable experience to those entering the parish ministry.

When a ministry demonstrates quality and substance it does not matter whether you are in a theater, warehouse or storefront, if you are providing rich grazing grounds for sheep they will find you. Integrity of heart and mind will foster and produce such a ministry. Define, clarify and highlight your vision in such a way that your followers are clear about your ministry, mandate and mission. When people are forced to second guess your vision, they tend to become tentative until further clarity comes. Secure leaders do not surround themselves with clones (persons who must think, act and resemble them). They find persons who can also identify their weaknesses as well as their strengths. My mentors never really brought up these concerns and issues!

For Dialogue and Reflection

1. To what extent are seminaries and Bible schools preparing future church leaders for twenty first century ministry challenges?

2. To what extent should we become pre-occupied with numerical quantitative factors in contrast to providing a qualitative Christian experience for converts?

3. Why is a trust relationship a necessary prerequisite for meaningful growth in today's church?

4. Discuss why insecure leaders surround themselves with clones (persons who think, act and resemble them) rather than individuals who can also identify their deficiencies.

Chapter

2   Monitor Your Front Door

Answer Only Seven.... Questions

1. *Did you know that 75% of most churches in North America average less than 140 persons in attendance?*

While this projection reflects a trend on the religious landscape of North America, it does not reflect trends globally. Exceptions would be in Asia, Africa and Latin America. Traditionally Korea was viewed as a strong Buddhist country. Today Korea is twenty-five percent Protestant and growing. There are about 45,000 churches in Korea, including some 6, 800 in Seoul. At least ten local churches in Seoul are classified as mega-churches with memberships over 30,000. [1] Hundreds of churches have memberships between 500 and 1,000. In West African countries such as Nigeria and Ghana several Christian mega churches have developed in the last decade. In Latin America the same holds true.

If your church numbers below 140 it is highly probable that you are classified with a significant portion of church fellowships across North America who gather weekly for worship, fellowship and service in the world. You are classified with a segment of yokepersons who seek to nurture and minister to millions of believers in diverse ways. Should you exceed this number, you will enter another phase of expansion in the life of your church.

The church of the twenty-first century must indeed seek newer forms of ministry as it ministers to a more diverse population, impacted by scientific and technological changes. Responsible meaningful church expansion will not simply focus on quantitative factors at the expense of qualitative factors. that are decisive in determining the effectiveness of a church's ministry. Remember if you focus on substance and quality the quantity will increase.

Too little information is available in assisting small to medium churches in maximizing their effectiveness. If you are a part of the seventy five percent of churches in North America who consist of one hundred forty persons or less and want to maximize your effectiveness, you are headed in the right direction. There are no magic formulas. But there are ways you can work smarter and less harder to maximize your effectiveness.

Whenever front door gains and back door loss are the same you have a problem

2. Is your back door (loss) as large as your front door (growth)?

Casually talk to the average pastor, regardless to the size of the congregation, if honest they will for the most part admit that back door loss is a persistent perennial problem. I have talked to ministers with 50 members and some with 500, and you are right, everybody admits that they are struggling with the same issue. Many will state that even during periods of significant expansion, without some meaningful plan to address causative factors related to loss, new members will depart as soon as they arrive. Are you plagued with the problem of wondering where are those new members who joined a few weeks ago? How many times have I heard pastors complain about the revolving door in their church and the ensuing frustrations that follow.

Back door loss has caused some of the most well intentioned pastors, once highly anointed and used by God, to throw up their hands in despair. Caring pastors who really love people are hurt when back door loss occurs. At least they want the privilege of conducting a back door interview when a member threatens to leave. If a member leaves without a valid reason, a caring pastor will view this as a serious matter. These dedicated servants of God see members as children of God, members of the community of faith endowed with divine peoplehood. Even the best of members may have valid reasons for leaving your church.

Compounding back door loss is the fact that our society continues to be mobile. Families move with job opportunities in the private, public and military sector. Families move further away from urban areas to escape what is perceived to be the rising tide of crime and other problems associated with the deterioration of the inner city. People will ordinarily move for what they perceive to be purely valid and legitimate reasons.

Even the best of members may have valid reasons for leaving your church

Compounding back door loss is the personality factor of congregation and pastor. There are many people in search of a church with a friendly personality even if they themselves are not friendly. The reasoning is that if we are out of sorts, we need to be in a church environment that is people-centered, friendly and organized. In several post-exit interviews conducted by yours truly, individuals cited non-acceptance as a factor in leaving. There are individuals who need a larger group of people to surround them in order to experience anonymity, the feeling of being non-discovered. There are persons who need a smaller setting where they can receive personal attention from a friendly congregation and pastor. When pastor and people are able to physically touch and interact with parishioners this often has value beyond words.

Sudden rapid changes in church programming can often become a point of tension for especially chronologically mature members who need a secure environment. Pastors should spend time laying the groundwork for rapid transitions in ministry programs. How often have I observed swift reactions to minor changes in worship format. Because religion is bound up with the emotions, religious change is more often the most difficult to accomplish.

Cliques or small power groups become dominant in the absence of strong leadership. Leaders should convey the message that they can be touched but not manipulated

Backdoor loss occurs when members do not feel involved in tasks where they can make significant contributions to the life and witness of the church. This problem is compounded when new comers get the feeling a clique is running the church. Cliques or small power groups become dominant in the absence of strong leadership. Pastoral leaders should convey the message that they can be touched, but not manipulated by any special interest group within the body.

I recalled announcing a change in direction of the church's larger vision and ministry, in the presence of unresolved tensions. Individuals who were affected by the unresolved tension used the former as an excuse to leave through the backdoor. Pastors need to understand that when members make up their minds to leave a ministry, no amount of coaxing or persuasion will suffice. There are instances when members are given the freedom to depart who by choice will remain. No member should leave without an exit interview. If members leave for the wrong reason they come under biblical condemnation that may lead to further bondage. Should members exit the backdoor with unresolved disputes or dissension the receiving pastor has a responsibility to send them back and clear the point of tension or engage in the act of reconciliation before proceeding with another ministry. Galatians [6:1] is still an excellent key for church discipline. The words of our blessed Lord in Matthew [18:15-20] holds the key to authentic reconciliation.

Revolving door loss can be minimized by pastoral leaders who are willing to share deeply matters of the heart and live with the sense that people are "the sheep of His pasture." We are managers and stewards entrusted for a brief moment with the task of nurturing God's people. You can rest assured that when revolving door loss equals front door gains, your congregation will remain the same size.

When a church remains the same size for fifteen years, all justified with an "eternal building fund," that church is in for a time of troubles. To be helped a leader of such a church must be open and honest and admit the need for assistance. Endemic problems will not just go away by mere wishing. Internal conflict, interpersonal tensions, disagreement on priorities, leadership struggle or a combination of other problems beneath the surface may contribute to the stunted growth and loss of members. George E. Hunter III's point is incisive:

"And it is also true that some congregational leadership lacks the Great Commission vision and will that can enable church growth. But clear and faithful preaching and teaching, combined with sharing the facts about the church and the community, can frequently awaken the vision and will." [2]

Church leaders, be encouraged, you are not far from the Kingdom, help is enroute. Pastors must be mature enough to understand that the time may come when a member may simply "self-destruct" by remaining with your church. On the other hand, some may leave and move on to greater maturity in their spiritual pilgrimage and walk with God. If we can be bold, self-critical and honest we might admit that there are some people who will not mature under our ministry. It may surprise you to know how many people are under our ministry who are not experiencing growth. If persons under our ministry are not growing they need to be moving on. We need to be honest, they need to be honest and realize they are not maturing.

Many Pastors will use coercion in getting members to stay. It is equally important that such persons find a ministry where they can mature. I have discovered that when you are open and honest with people the Lord respects that. I am convinced after years of trial and failure there are ways that your back door loss (attrition rate) can be addressed. You can permanently lock the back door of your church, and make sure all side exits are secure.

MAXIMIZE YOUR POTENTIAL

3. Would you like to see your church identify its actual growth potential, and then develop a strategy to achieve it?

This book will help you to identify your growth potential. Once you identify same, there are strategies to help you grow. According to the great Greek philosopher Aristotle, an acorn is a potential oak tree. When you hold a tiny acorn in your hand, it certainly does not feel or look like an oak tree. But that tiny little acorn is loaded with all that constitutes an oak tree. That ingredient is called potential. A process has to occur in order to move a thing from its potential state to its actual. Allow your church to be that tiny little acorn, bursting with the possibility to become.

A seed must experience a process called germination. That process is dependent upon the sun, moisture, wind and the force of nature to come to bear upon the tiny seed. It is a long way from being an oak tree, but you can rest assured it is in a process of becoming. My purpose is to assist you in selectively identifying all the factors present in your church environment that are awaiting the process of spiritual germination.

Once those dormant causative factors are identified and lifted up for examination, you will then be ready to develop an expansion strategy. There is no one way to become an oak tree for God's Kingdom. There are several expansion and development strategies, but they all coalesce into one single goal...to become an oak tree for the purpose of God's Kingdom. So, relax and tell yourself, I may be an acorn now but I am in the process of becoming...a giant oak for God. The word potential means "possible but not yet realized; capable of being but not yet in existence; latent." It means the inherent ability or capacity for growth, development, or coming into being."

When intangible factors such as courage, fearlessness, esteem, and trust combine with tangibles, your potential can become actualized. How often as pastors we face projects that appear to be within reason, but the ingredient to make it go was missing. The freedom to innovate is not always a luxury.

That is when we can best discover the function of the Holy Spirit as an enabler. As an enabler the Holy Spirit can assist us in marshaling the right set of facts, assumptions and intangibles so that they connect with tangible factors that will bring to fruition frustrated dreams.

Do not despair because your plans for the expansion of your ministry is on hold and embryonic. As in the case of a pre-born child, all the genetic information for a total person is strangely concealed in the tiny blob of jelly like protoplasm obscure in the womb. What is going to come of all of this? Time and circumstance are the final arbiter's of the enormous hope concealed in the womb. Babies do not arrive on *chronos* [mere clock time], but rather on *"Kairos,"* a greek term for time pregnant and charged with meaning. We are more than mere flotsam and jetsam [discarded cargo] on the sea of time. Ultimately God has the final say about when, where and how our ministries will expand and mature. *"The harvest truly is plenteous,"* says the Master..

Why not Brighten the Corners .... Within Your Community
4. *Do you believe that your church could minister more effectively if you were able to identify and respond to the unique challenges in your community?*

In every community where churches are found unique challenges are also present. Most times these challenges are right under our nose. Our urban centers are laden with social dynamite. With the teeming growth of major cities comes specific social problems booming at an alarming rate. Near us are lonely golden agers, alienated youth, street people, the ever present problem of hunger and psychological and social dysfunction. Police brutality, dual standards of justice within our criminal justice system, slum housing, inadequate health care, all are troubling signs of the time. Added to this is the ever present problem of class and racism. While racism represents the most extreme form of organized domination and dehumanization yet devised, it is crucial to note that the most profound indignities in American life continue to be reserved for people of color. [3]

Discernment is important in identifying specific challenges within your community. Challenges, when processed correctly, help us grow and mature in the Lord. As you respond to initial challenges and become responsive to people needs the Lord will begin to send people who have needs you can meet. I shall never forget the challenge that was next to our church. We were so busy having church we missed an opportunity to save a soul and several lives. The challenge began when a new family moved next to our church in a rental flat. No one made contact with this family. We would speak out of courtesy and continue with business as usual. The challenge erupted into a crises two hours past our Sunday worship. The father who had been unemployed took a rifle, wounded his infant son, fatally wounded his common-law wife and committed suicide This incident became the turning point for our congregation's outreach to our immediate community. This even became the basis for a presentation at a mission conference in Ventnor, New Jersey, where I argued a case for evangelization and liberation.

While evangelization deals with the tools and techniques for reaching the lost, liberation has to do with freeing persons from the various bondages that we can become subject to in this world. For in every "crisis" is an opportunity to creatively respond. As disciples of our blessed Lord, we are commanded to share the good news of what He has done for us with others (Matthew 28:18-20). There must be lines of communication between the church and the community in which it is located. Start now to identify the unique challenges right at your front door.

Too often, challenges for ministry are like a coral snake, vibrant in color, so much like the landscape they become camouflaged, hidden - but deadly. Traditionally, in seminary we spend countless hours training individuals for the missionary enterprise abroad, and this has its merits. The church in North America must conquer the challenges at home. When our neighborhoods are so crime-ridden that it is unsafe for people to congregate at church, the church is challenged. When family disintegration takes place at a far too rapid rate within neighborhood and church, the church is challenged. When we lose our youth to the streets in declining neighborhoods, the church is challenged.

A crisis is a crucial point or situation in the course of anything. The Greek word *krisis* from which the Latin word crisis is derived, also means opportunity. With all the challenges impending within our communities, this can be the church's finest hour. God has a peculiar pattern of showing up in the midst of crucial times, in order to display His power. The church must be more than a physician that only gives diagnosis and prognosis, it must become preventive and prescriptive for the social and spiritual maladies of our times. To be effective the church must assume the servant role in order to achieve maximum effectiveness.

Avoid Placing Dreams on Hold

5. Is your vision of ministry on hold for lack of resources?

Resources may very well be spiritual as well as material. For many church leaders the challenge is not lack of vision, but rather resources. "Without a vision the people perish," is the biblical admonition. Without the resources, the vision will diminish. In other situations, the financial resources are present but are grossly mishandled, thus jeopardizing the vision. I have observed small churches that were well managed accomplished gargantuan tasks while large churches with many resources failed to accomplish small tasks.

It is fairly common knowledge in church circles that there are few churches that boast of being a one hundred percent tithing church. Most churches tithe about twenty to thirty percent, while seventy to eighty percent of untapped financial resource potential is just sitting there waiting to happen. The untapped financial potential will not become actualized unless it is cultivated and developed. While the goal of each pastor should be to develop a one hundred percent tithing church, should you succeed with seventy percent, it will be enough to match your vision of ministry.

The purpose of the tithe is to underwrite the total ministries of the church

Once your congregation is steeped in biblical stewardship that emphasizes the rationale for giving, i.e., "we do not give in order to be blessed, but rather because we are blessed," your church's response will change for the better. Once the resources begin to grow consistently, you can accomplish any financial objective you set. Should you desire to purchase church vans, expansion of educational ministries, underwriting part-time or full-time staff, expanding present facilities or purchasing land, the resources will be present. The purpose of the tithe is to underwrite the total ministry of the church.

From here on in, perk up, as you trust the Lord to move upon His people so that they will come to see and understand their special role in underwriting the vision. God is waiting to give the increase to His servants who can trust His faithfulness (Lamentation 3:22-23 NIV). *"For His compassion never fail. They are new every morning great is your faithfulness."*

6. Is Intercessory Prayer Foundational to Your Ministry?

Intercessory prayer redeems us from trusting our wisdom. It is our "cloud" by day and our " pillar of fire" by night. I have learned after several attempts of trial and failure at some tasks, that intercessory prayer must be foundational to whatever we attempt to do. Intercession as an act on our behalf is important at all times. Prayer should not be an act attached to your ministry, it must be foundational. Those who honor God are also honored by Him. The record reveals that when a church engages in consistent intercessory prayer, the potential for doing God's will is always present.

According to the biblical record those persons used by God from Abraham to Daniel knew the significance of intercession. To intercede is to pray on behalf of another. Jesus Christ is our primary example. (NIV, I Timothy 2:5), "For there is one God and one mediator between God and men, the man Jesus Christ, who gave himself as a ransom for all men." Someone has reminded us that "prayerless pews make powerless pulpits." What we are attempting for God is indeed spiritual. It is possible to become so engrossed in a task utilizing human ingenuity that we forget that we are working for God on behalf of His Kingdom in the earth.

Intercessory prayer accomplishes several important things for leaders who desire to expand their ministries for God. Evelyn Underhill defines prayer as "turning to reality, taking our part, however humble, tentative and half-understood, in the continual conversation, the communion, of our spirits with the Eternal Spirit. . . . for prayer is really our whole life toward God: our longing for Him, our "incurable God-sickness," as Barth calls it, our whole drive towards Him.[4] In order for a church's ministry to secure necessary grounding, intercessory prayer must not be an option. Constant intercessory prayer accomplishes several things. Intercessory prayer unites, reconciles and sustains.

1). Intercessory prayer unites. Consistent intercessory prayer on behalf of the pastoral vision has a tendency to unite church members even in the presence of petty tensions and conflicts. My continual interaction with Pastor John and Neicy Outen, of the Strong Tower Church of God In Christ of Moreno Valley, California has borne witness to the significance of consistent intercessory prayer , solid Bible study and a meaningful worship service as a force for impacting people. I predict a great future for this church should it remain faithful. Plans are underway to build a sanctuary in a valley exploding with new population. Intercessory prayer creates a unique sense of congregational esprit de corps, as those things that divide us become diminished in the presence of the Lord. Intercessory prayer for the vision will cause those things that are opposed to the vision to "grow strangely dim" in the light of God's glory and grace.

(2) Intercessory prayer reconciles. Henri J. M. Nouwen, in ***With Open Hands***, gets to the heart of the matter when he candidly states "the question of when or how to pray is not really the most important one. The crucial question is whether you should pray always and whether your prayer is necessary. Here, the stakes are all or nothing" [5]

Biblical reconciliation involves removal of barriers which divide. A pastoral vision comes under attack long before it is shared. Every vision of ministry reveals the heart of God for that particular congregation. Somewhere I read "Satan trembles at the weakest saint upon his/her knees." The walls that divide must crumble in the presence of persistent intercessory prayer for the pastoral vision. (3) Intercessory Prayer sustains. In the Gospel of Matthew [18:19-20], the words of Jesus, *"Again I say unto you, that is two of you shall agree on earth as touching anything that they shall ask, it shall be done for them of my Father which is in heaven."* All too often pastoral leaders experience a roller coaster effect with pastoral vision. One month the vision appears to be within reach, the next month they have all but given up. Such vacillation can wreak havoc upon the people of God.

The pastoral vision will be sustained as intercessors touch and agree for it. Intercessory prayer encourages us to be patient as we wait for God. Pastor Kirk Baxter of Cathedral of Love COGIC, Willingboro, N.J., sponsors an annual prayer weekend to enhance the spiritual life of his parishioners. Recently, National Evangelist Judy Shaw Roberson of Sioux Falls South Dakota conducted such an event.

7. *Would you like to widen the front door and close the back door of your church by maximizing your effectiveness and actualizing your potential?*

Most pastors would like to become more effective in their ministry. The fact that you are reading this book indicates that you are already numbered among those who want to maximize their effectiveness by actualizing their potential by simply opening the front door and closing the back door of your church. To do so requires commitment and persistence on your part. It means to become goal centered and focused. Those who fail to plan are invariably planning to fail. Inability to plan is a sign of poor stewardship of time and a misuse of valuable resources.

Every church has the potential for substantial growth provided certain tangible and intangible factors come together. There are scores of unchurched people that could be reached with the Gospel by ministries that are prepared to reap the harvest. A basic goal of our discourse is to assist small to medium congregations to increase and expand under optimum environmental conditions. To attain such a goal requires a review of what may be categorized as side door issues since they can also attract and repel newcomers. When we review the statistics highlighting ineffective churches it gives us a reason to hope. I came across this anonymous statistic:

5% of reported church members do not exist
10% cannot be found
20% never pray
25% never read the Bible
30% never attend church
40% never give to any cause
50% never go to Sunday School
60% never attend Sunday evening service
70% never give to missions
75% never engage in any church activities
80% never go to prayer meeting
90% never have family worship
95% never win a soul to Christ

If this statistic has any validity it raises serious questions about the nature of the church and its purpose for being. To develop an effective ministry requires time and productive planning. Such are the radical demands of the Kingdom of God.

For Dialogue and Reflection

1. Is it necessary to conduct post exit interviews for departing members?

2. How does one handle members who leave for the wrong reasons?

3. Have you identified unique challenges in your immediate community?

4. Is intercessory prayer necessary in an expanding ministry?

chapter
3
Making the Front Door the Right Door

A Winning Combination: Word and Deed

To be meaningful, qualitative church expansion must be grounded in scripture, or it can easily degenerate into a numbers game. Etched in my memory is the warm summer afternoon while working in my church study, when suddenly I heard a knock at the door. Within seconds I was face to face with a middle-aged, Anglo-American gentleman from suburban Glendale, who admonished me that God had sent him to talk to me about personal soul-winning. After my initial screening process, I asked him whether he realized he was on the borderline of Watts. As the conversation progressed, I was directed to a passage in the book of Daniel (12:3) *"...And they that be wise shall shine as the brightness of the firmament: and they that turn many to righteousness as the stars forever and ever."*

I now confess that I had spent countless hours in the book of Daniel, pre-occupied with creatively describing Daniel's deliverance from the lion's den or convincing the audience of the exemplary power of God brought to bear in God's mighty deliverance of the Hebrew boys from the fiery furnace. I had callously overlooked this scriptural gem tucked away in Daniel 12:3. In it is found an implicit challenge to become a super star for God by becoming involved in the process of "turning many to righteousness."

I was directed to Luke 14:23 to rediscover anew another diamond tucked away in verse 23... *"Go into the highway and hedges and compel them to come in that my house may be filled."* In preaching on the parable of the Great Supper, my focus had been on the primary invitees who had refused the initial invitation by rendering plausible excuses. Upon close examination of the parable, none of the three had valid excuses. A supper would have been a delightful place for a newly wedded couple; few people would purchase land without knowing the full dimension of it; and rarely would anyone purchase oxen without a thorough examination of each animal.

The stranger in my office went on to further admonish me to prepare a feast and invite the poor because God has a special concern for them. Throughout the Old Testament God demonstrated an overwhelming concern for widows, orphans, and the poor so that they would not be victimized by an unjust social system. We responded by preparing a feast without charge, and that was the beginning of a fruitful harvest of souls. I never heard from or saw this stranger again. In hindsight he may have been an angel.

Revival and Evangelism: Similar But Different

When the time of harvest occurs, it is crucial that the people of God understand the critical distinction between revival and evangelism. Evangelism has to do with the methods and techniques that we utilize in the process of leading persons to Christ. Most Christian book stores have sections describing the master plan of evangelism. Evangelism is inclusive of those human techniques that we use under divine guidance. Revival means to give life to that which is dead. Revival is exclusively a work of the Holy Spirit encountering us in unique ways breathing life upon valleys laden with dry bones. It is possible to have so many meetings that you can find yourself coming from meetings and not experience revival.

Revival does not occur apart from genuine repentance on the part of those who long for it. The term revival is consistently found throughout the Old Testament. What a strange irony that Jesus came preaching repentance. The Greek word "metanoia" best renders the true meaning of the term, "change of heart, mind and direction." Jesus was the Kingdom of God personalized. When he admonishes us to repent for the Kingdom of Heaven is at hand, it becomes a serious matter for the church to take heed. I honestly believe that when the church takes seriously the mandate to repent, indeed the Kingdom will break through. It will not break through in its fullness over recalcitrant unrepentant sins. It may surprise and shock us to know the kinds of things that repel the Kingdom. The little foxes of pettiness nibble away at the vines.

To overlook and disrespect the humanity of others, to nurse and carry grudges month after month, are the kinds of things that hinder the divine spiritual encounter we call revival. Second Chronicles 7:14, continues to have relevance for the whole people of God. *"If my people which are called by my name will humble themselves, pray and seek my face then will I hear from heaven I will forgive their sins, and heal their land."* When the community of faith repents, it too experiences the freshness of forgiveness which prepares us for those things that come to us through God's special gift of salvation through Jesus Christ alone.

In the act of forgiveness from the divine side, God relieves us of our sense of guilt, so that we are no longer imprisoned. Guilt fractures human personality in the long run, creates anxiety, depression and havoc in the human heart. From the biblical perspective,"godly sorrow worketh repentance." Divine forgiveness means relationship restored. The fetters are snapped, the barriers are down, the scapegoats can be released and returned to the wilds, for restoration has come. Our sins are forgiven (Ephesians 4:32), blotted out (Isaiah 44:22), covered (Psalm 85:2), removed (Psalm 103:12), cast into the sea (Micah 7:19), hid (Hosea 12:12), hid behind God's back (Isaiah 38:17), forgotten (Isaiah 43:25), never to be mentioned (Ezekiel 33:16).

Authentic revival does not occur apart from radical genuine repentance

When we who comprise His church repent throughout our ranks, do not be surprised when revival breaks through and the Holy Spirit comes like a mighty rushing wind. Our Lord speaks through John in his vision on Patmos to admonish the seven churches to repent or radical consequences would take place. The Welsh Revival at the turn of the century (1904) in England under the leadership of Evan Roberts, a young pastor, began in a call to repentance and an earnest quest for God. Currents from the Welsh Revival flowed across the Atlantic Ocean into the spiritual milieu that prepared the way for the Los Angeles Azusa Street Revival of 1906 led by William J. Seymour. Revivals like thunderstorms do not just happen. Certain pre-conditions must precede revivals. Isaiah [40:3] ff. provides an excellent biblical word for the form in which true spiritual renewal takes place. The voice that crieth, in verse 3 & 4 is the call to repentance that prepares the way of the Lord. In verse four, there is a leveling, a straightening, a smoothing, a revealing and a seeing process. Are we ready to weep between the porch and the altar? The prophet Jeremiah made an urgent plea for the "mourning women" to come and begin "wailing" on behalf of the community of faith [Jer. 9:17]. When the warm air currents collide with cold air currents, the results can be violent thunderstorms. So it is with revivals born of the Spirit.

When the Gospel is presented with convicting power, people will hear the voice of the Lord as a call to penitence. The human spirit comes under the mighty sway and power of the Holy Spirit and makes that which is ordinary, extraordinary. The pattern of Pentecost must prevail if revival is to be authentic. They were united in prayer and praise all with one accord [Acts 1:14]; their actions were based on their understanding of prophecy transmitted through the Scripture [Acts 1:16, 20]. They were assembled together in one place [Acts 2:1]; There was the outpouring of the Holy Spirit [Acts 2:2-4]; There was proclamation [Acts 2:14-36]; there was conviction and repentance [Acts 2:37, 38]; there was mutual sharing [Acts 2:44-45]; there was continuity with the tradition in a new way [Acts 2:46]; and then came the results [Acts 2:47].

We are only ready for authentic revival when we accept the fact that it is exclusively and ultimately a work of the Spirit. Meetings alone will not guarantee revival. Meetings alone will not raise the dead. A breathless body is a lifeless body. In Ezekiel's vision of the valley of dry, bleached disinterred bones, the wind of God which is the symbol of the Spirit must not only blow upon these bones, but must enter into them and create life in the presence of death.

Even the prophet Ezekiel makes the admission that only God could resurrect the bones. God does enlist the prophet's participation by commanding him to prophesy, to set forth God's claim, to speak the word of proclamation to these bones. Then the unprecedented miracle of transformation occurs - the boneyard comes alive. There can be no life in our contemporary churches apart from divine breath. Too much of what is labeled revival today is cosmetic.

Our best human endeavors will come to naught unless we come to understand that they must be launched guided and sustained by the Holy Spirit. The Holy Spirit as God, is indispensable. Our best spiritually fashioned human methods of resuscitation will not create and sustain life in our pews. Alas, we must plead, "Spirit of the living God, fall afresh on us."

Why Dynamic Worship is Magnetic

An uninspiring, unfruitful worship service may be due to lack of focus and planning. However a few myths need to be dispelled. A quiet reverential worship is not necessarily a dead worship. A worship where the audience does not say Amen after each spoken word is not necessarily a dead worship. In order for a worship service to be alive and magnetic it must indeed be God-centered. Our Lord sets the requirements for true worship in his conversation with the woman of Samaria recorded in John 4: "*God is a Spirit and they that worship Him must worship Him in spirit and in truth.*" Music alone does not create worship. Numbers do not make worship. When Jesus Christ is the center of attraction, worship exudes beauty and quiet strength. Jesus alone is to be worshiped in majesty. It is the element of majesty that becomes the point of contact and attraction for persons seeking the sheltering atmosphere of a church home.

A dead worship is not necessarily one with a worship format or plan. In some worship traditions if you follow the written program too closely, you will be viewed as having "lost the Spirit." There may be an element of truth in that myth that needs heeding. Evelyn Underhill's definition of worship as "the soul's response to God" is still meaningful. Everything we do or utilize is only a means of pointing us toward the true object of our worship. The worship plan must become integrated into the flow of our response to God to the point that we move from it to Him. According to the Psalmeth "*in His presence is fullness of joy.*"

The worship plan is intended to be the vehicle that moves us in the realm of the Spirit where adoration and wonder, delight and glory flourishes. People will travel distances to participate in a unique worship. Whatever critique we may have of the recent Toronto Blessing Revival and the Pensacola Revival, there is something happening that merits attention. Our critique must go beyond form to substance. There is something within each of us that is attracted to that which is authentic and real.

When the church is focused on meeting real human needs at the social, spiritual and personal level in a holistic way, it becomes magnetic. A Christo-centric church with a praise - centered worship combined with internal and external ministries that engages the whole person, becomes an attractive option. Such a church becomes attractive because the angle of vision is correct, the vision is clear, the mandate and mission are focused. When the church makes a statement by what it does rather than what it calls itself or its cosmetic make-up, it is ready for relevant witness to God's glory and this alone is totally attractive.

"I was glad when they said unto me let us go into the house of the Lord", the words of the Psalmist bear witness to our spirit in our quest for the authentic and our at homeness with the Community of faith.

Ritual has to do with what we do within worship as an act of worship. Ritual within worship has to do with the way we appropriate symbols. Ritual appears to be natural to humankind. At the basis of worship lies the formalization of natural actions, expressed in corporate gatherings of adoration, praise and thanksgiving to God in response to His activity in the world. A symbol points to a reality beyond itself. When the ritual is so overwhelming and dominating that the object of worship becomes diminished, worship loses its meaning. When our use of symbols becomes a thing in itself, worship becomes merely cultic. Even our worship can become idolatrous if it is not theocentric.

The God we worship is jealous and desires our total commitment. The soul does not respond to God within a vacuum. Such a response must take place within a context, and for those who serve God, worship is the context. *A good worship leader must have a special "eye" for seeing and a special "ear" for hearing and discerning the mind of the Spirit for the immediate worshiping moment.*

The context of worship must be of such that the soul can respond to the Creator in authentic freedom. That is why worship as an act of celebration is crucially important. A focused worship is geared toward authentic celebration. Anyone should not lead worship. Worship leaders should be carefully chosen and given significant guidance. The act of worship requires discernment. The worship leader must have a special "eye" for seeing and a special "ear" for hearing the mind of the Spirit for the immediate worshiping movement. A callous non-discerning worship leader can lead to a disastrous worship service.

A good worship leader guides persons in the act of worship. Churches who invest resources and energy in improving the context of worship will draw rather than repel. There are few events as beautiful as a worship service that is related. The leader makes sure the prayer is related to the Scripture, and Scripture is related to songs of praise in a given worship. The element of relatedness sets the context for worship. The element of relatedness leads to unity within the context of worship. When a worshiping congregation lifts a united voice toward the throne of God, heaven comes down and glory is made manifest.

A good worship leader guides persons participating in the act of worship away from themselves and the mundane

A good worship leader guides persons participating in the act of worship away from themselves and the mundane. God is not glorified when symbol is confused with subject; God is not glorified when shadow is confused with substance. God is not glorified when ritual becomes central. *"To glorify God and enjoy Him forever,"* must be the goal and focus of true worship. When God is central to worship, angels ascend and descend as the Creator and Sustainer of all life is adored. If the context of worship is not subject to biblical theological critique, it runs the risk of becoming *"staid," "canned"* and irrelevant.

The primary task of theology is to clarify the nature of the Christian faith. Telling [word] and doing [deed] appears to have been characteristic of early Christian worship as recorded in Acts 2:42 *"And they devoted themselves to the Apostle's teaching and fellowship, to the breaking of bread and the prayers."* Not only did they pray, but they broke bread in full celebration around the Lord's Table. The biblical model of sharing the word, prayers and bread is timeless. It transcends fixed momentary times. [I Cor. 11:24-25] - *"This do in remembrance of me...as often as ye drink it in remembrance of me."* Worship too is timeless.

When that which is timeful, is placed within the context of that which is timeless, it takes on new meaning. That is why the context of worship is so crucial to understand and embrace. Karl Barth the renown Swiss Protestant theologian stated, *"Christian worship is the most momentous, the most urgent, the most glorious action that can take place in the human life."* Whether your worship is traditional Protestant, liturgical, contemporary or in the praise and worship tradition, it is central, foundational and primary to all that we do. Metaphorically, worship is the body of water that feeds the smaller streams and rivulets, each important in its own way. If the main body of water suffers contamination, it fouls the streams, rivulets and brooks. That is why true worship transcends places. Whether it takes place in a cotton field or cathedral, it should be given primacy because it informs whatever else we do. The term worship by way of Middle English signifies "worthship." To engage in the act of worship is to declare God's worth.

The late Dr. Samuel Proctor, Pastor Emeritus of Abyssinian Baptist Church, Harlem, premiere Dean of Black Preaching in our time, commenting on Christian worship as *"the adoration and praise of God and the exercise of seeking communion with God, privately or corporately, in a cathedral or in a tent, in a temple or an open field, at home or in a store front."¹* When worship is reduced to charismania comedy, where ego-boosting, and self-aggrandizing hype is the order of the day, the chloroform treatment might result in a healthier church body in general. Worship is not ancillary to what we do, it is the "prime mover" for whatever other ministries may be in place.

Worship should not be perceived as a "fix" for all of our maladies and egotistical wants. There are persons who go from church to church seeking a "fix" for their pain and problems. They must constantly resist the temptation of becoming "religious junkies" and substitute it for being a "fool for Christ." Authentic worship is encounter. Through the medium of worship the living God encounters us at the deepest level of our humanity. Worship then becomes the vehicle of transformation and not manipulation.

Our society has been afflicted with the syndrome of overstimulation. We depend upon other people and things to stimulate us because we cannot bear to be alone. The realization of the presence of God is the key to understanding joy which is permanent, while happiness is occasional and may require a "fix." When worship is authentic other functions of ministry flow from its stream.

During the ante-bellum period worship provided the necessary empowerment to oppose an evil and unjust order that perpetrated oppression because of race

Is it any wonder that the presence of the African-American church in North America through the medium of worship gave credence to the struggle for rights and privileges accorded by the constitution, but denied them in reality on the basis of color. Worship provided the necessary empowerment to oppose an evil and unjust social order that perpetrated oppression because of race. Worship in the slave master's church did not provide the security and freedom enjoyed within what slaves perceived to be the "Invisible Institution," far away from the watchful eyes of white people.²

The evolvement of Black Methodism in North America was initiated within a racially divided church, St. George Episcopal Church, and protested by Richard Allen and company. The Modern Civil Rights Movement received its greatest impetus from the African-American church at worship that produced a Martin Luther King and other church persons who provided leadership. It is in worship that we encounter and are encountered by the living God. In worship we not only respond to God, but we enter into communion with our Creator. Intimate communion with God transforms us in ways that defy imagination, according to Hebrews 12:29. *"Our God is a consuming fire."* The practice of sinning will snuff out the volatility of divine fire, likewise the flame of His presence will burn the dross and purge sin from the inner recesses of our being.

Tradition is merely the medium through which the divine appears to us. It is not the only medium. I have deep appreciation for Jaroslav Pelican's wisdom regarding tradition which he sees as *"the living faith of the dead passed on from one generation to another via customs and beliefs." Traditionalism is the dead faith of the living assigned the status of divine revelation."* How often do we see worship strained because traditionalism is confused with tradition and becomes the order of the day. When worship must be done a certain way to uphold a tradition that no longer has relevance, the church gets into trouble.

Within the Jewish tradition, the God-encounter is rooted in a sense of awe and enshrouded in a deep sense of mystery. An encounter with the "Numinous" must always be clothed in mystery. For the central paradox of Jewish theology is: that God is seen and yet not seen, known and yet unknowable, revealed but always in hiddenness and obscurity. The knowledge of God is a dark knowledge, a knowledge which involves the encounter with the unutterable.....there is a sense in which the mystery must be preserved by the discretion of human speech. [3]

When the worship experience is reduced to a momentary "fix" we miss its real meaning

It is not uncommon in praise and worship traditions to hear popular coined sayings such as, "when praises go up, blessings come down. " When we worship for the express purpose of receiving special benefits from God, worship can readily become a tool for manipulation. When the worship experience becomes a "fix" we miss its real meaning. We should focus on the substance of the experience and not merely the experience itself. We worship God purely for the sake of worshiping God and for who He is. Black worship is valid insofar as God is approached without "form and fashion" but in simplicity and sincerity.[4]

Our worship practices and claims should stand the test of theology. The issue is not theology or non-theology, but rather good theology or bad theology. Even theology must be subject to the scrutiny of Scripture. There are many religious communities in our world embracing claims that are aberrant and arrogant, unwilling to subject themselves to scrutiny of any kind. When Jim Jones led over 900 persons to their death in Guyana, 1978, David Koresh in Waco, Texas, and more recently the HeavensGate fiasco in San Diego, all operated under the banner of the Christian faith, leading followers in the act of worship. [Revelation 5:12, 13-14] *"Blessings and honor, and glory, and power, be unto him that sitteth upon the throne, and unto the Lamb forever and ever. The four and twenty elders fell down and worshiped Him that liveth for ever and ever."*

A magnetized object exerts powerful and irresistible influence upon similar objects. Not only are we admonished to *"sing praises unto God,"* but to *"worship the Lord in the beauty of holiness."* When we enthusiastically enter into God's presence with high praise, it is attractive. Bob Sorge makes a rather telling point as he differentiates between worshiping and the worshiper. He suggests that anyone can worship as the occasion might demand without coming under the discipline, commitment and life-style of a worshiper.

According to Sorge: *"God knows we must do other things besides vocalize our worship. But God does ask us to live a life consistent with that of a worshiper seven days a week.....we will begin to realize that everything we do truly constitutes an act of worship unto the Lord."* [5]

Music is an important component of worship in most churches. The use of hymns, sacred, traditional and contemporary music, appropriately provides an attractive option. James White presents seven categories as points of reference in a Protestant worship service. They are as follows: people, piety, time, place, prayer, preaching, and music. [6] Each category taken serious can provide an attractive challenge for those who are weary and are thirsting for God.

A church can become an ecclesiastical showcase of some bygone era unless it is willing to undergo change

Be Open to Change

In a world impacted by rapid radical social change, what are we to do as the church in the world? What ought to be the nature of our response? Museums are built primarily for displaying art or some relic of the past. Large sums of money are appropriated annually to preserve artifacts of the past. A church can become an ecclesiastical showcase of some bygone era unless it is willing to change. Huge reptiles of the ancient past are mute testimony to those who are unwilling to undergo change. A paradigm is an example serving as a pattern, a model, a prototype, a replica, a standard, a norm, a representation.

The church in North America and on several continents has experienced unprecedented growth during this century. Africa, Asia and South America have witnessed a spectacular response to Christianity in the last three decades. How to be a Christian in a non-Christian world continues to be a challenge to the Christian church. As we enter the twenty-first century, we are encountering new secular challenges.

During the fall of 1992, Time magazine produced a special issue, titled, Beyond the Year 2000, what to expect in the millennium. A byline for the article entitled, the Astonishing 20th Century, states, for good and ill, people of our time have witnessed more change than anyone who ever lived." In perusing the table of contents for this special issue, I found it most revealing in attempting to describe a future yet to be. With respect to the century ahead, the following captions are highly revelatory. Into the Unknown, the future will be complex, fast-paced and turbulent. Will we be ready?; Seeking Other Worlds, technology will bring a new space age. Will we find anybody out there? Higher Tech, here comes intelligent machines, multisensual media and highly evolved artificial creatures, The Family Network, the loosely knit clan of the future won't be at all like the Jetsons., The New World Order, with militarism leveling, all the big questions will be basically economic., The Love Connection, sex and dating will be attempted only by thrill seekers; The Age of Genetics (the success of the recent sheep cloning experiment), it could rival the Industrial Revolution.; Learning Leap, education will have to become a central theme of American life.; No Breathing Room, can the earth support 11 billion people?; Video Deluge, the choices will dazzle, but will the heart be lonely?; Revelations, Faith will thrive, theology will suffer. [7]

Should faith thrive and theology suffer in the coming millennium, the challenges for a new paradigm shift are obvious. In times of rapid cultural change, a crisis of images is to be expected, says, Avery Dulles. Many traditional images have lost their former hold on people, while the new images have not yet had time to gain their full power, all contributing to what Dulles views as the contemporary crisis of faith, which is in very large part, a crisis of images.[8] When a model becomes dominant, it can be labeled a paradigm. When a model proves to be successful in solving a great variety of problems and becomes a tool for unraveling anomalies as yet unsolved, it rises to the status of a paradigm.[9]

It was Thomas S. Kuhn, who from a scientific context gave credence to the term, "paradigm." For Kuhn, paradigms are "concrete puzzle - solutions which, employed as models or examples, can replace explicit rules as a basis for the solution of the remaining puzzles of normal science."[10]

While a paradigm shift is needed for churches facing the 21st century, we must take precaution and understand that while paradigms are important, they are relative. Since each paradigm brings with it, its own special images, commitment, rhetoric, values and priorities, in its transition from one to another, with it comes to a particular set of problems. Dulles is insightful, careful to note, "when paradigms shift, people suddenly find the ground cut from under their feet." Such persons, cannot begin to speak the new language without already committing themselves to a whole new set of values that may not be to their taste. Thus they find themselves gravely threatened in their spiritual security. [11]

Change, we must, not for change sake, but for relevance as we communicate to a population that has been impacted by modernity and social change. Undergirding our deep spiritual insecurity is a thirst and quest for the divine. The impact of New Age philosophy has impacted major institutions among us. A 900 number can get your horoscope read with promise of the right spouse. The upsurge of interest led by Hollywood's finest in crystals, channeling and reincarnation are bold neon signs announcing a strong desire and quest for the supernatural. One sees the return to a spiritual quest among baby busters.

Leaders must undergo a paradigm shift in order to clearly delineate the differences between religiosity and authentic christian encounter with Jesus Christ. We must be prepared in clear apologetic tones to remind those who are thirsty that religion is the human quest for the divine, while in authentic christian encounter, God is always in search of lost humanity. Wickedness is on the rampage in our time.

As we approach the millenium there will be an increase in the occult and the rise of new cults. As people seek for security and meaning religion will not be without its rivals. Religious movements with political agendas will also increase. There are those who are bent on ushering in theocratic rule by infiltrating the government. Such patterns are not new in church history. Those for whom religion is a mere "fix" and who do not know the meaning of struggle may be postured or set up for disillusionment. Pastors, leaders, church officials, get ready? Our time has come!

Chapter

4 This Key Works...the Master Speaks

Expanding His Kingdom in the World

To find the secret of mastery, you need a Master. The Master mastered persons into masterfulness.....Mastery is primarily caught not taught. Mastery is gained by contact with the Master. To be masterful you must get in touch with the resources of a Master. The dictionary defines a master as one who has become proficient , a person of consummate skill in an art, technique.[1] In the martial arts, a Master is one who knows all there is to know about fighting. When the Master speaks we are compelled to listen.

Ultimately, it is Jesus, who is the Christ, who is building His church. (Matthew 16:18-19)*"And I say unto thee, that thou art Peter, and upon this rock I will build my church and the gates of hell shall not prevail against it. And I will give unto thee the keys of the kingdom of Heaven....."* These momentous words were spoken to Cephas, whose name means rock or stone. the rock upon which Jesus would build his church has been a subject of debate for centuries. There are those who contend that the rock refers to Peter, the first great leader of the church at Jerusalem, and leader of the Apostolic band. There are those who contend that the rock refers either to Jesus himself, or to the confession of faith given by Peter.

The former posture tends to be supported by the Catholic interpretation of Peter as the first head of the church on earth, and is the leader of Apostolic succession. The latter view tends to be embraced by Protestant Orthodoxy, with the belief that Peter's confession of faith would be embraced by all subsequent true believers in every age. In (I Peter 2:4-6), the Apostle himself reminds Christians that " they are the church built on the foundation of the Apostles and Prophets with Jesus Christ as the Chief Cornerstone." Were the church based solely on Peter, his failures alone would have decided the course of the role of the church in history. Some denominations have been birthed on this notion alone.

Likewise, verse 19, has been a subject of debate for centuries. There are those who contend that the *"Keys of the Kingdom of Heaven,"* means the authority to implement church discipline and the power to forgive sins. There are those who contend that the "Keys" represent a symbolic statement for those who may through the door of opportunity lead persons into the Kingdom by presenting the claims of the Gospel. While there may be merit to both postures, we can be reasonably sure that no human person has the power to literally keep anyone out of the Kingdom of Heaven, if they have faith in Jesus Christ our Supreme Lord and Master.

The problem that plagues contemporary Christianity this final quarter of the twentieth century is that too many of us are attempting to build "His" church apart from "His" authority and guidance. The issue is not that of the vast proliferation of churches that crowd our city blocks. A noted theologian suggested during the close of a lecture in Tulsa , 1993 that some of these small churches might consider closing down and combining their strength with churches in similar situations in order to become formidable. The issue has to do with what kinds of churches do we have? Do these churches truly belong to Jesus Christ, the Master?

Our world is viewed as a global village due to the increasingly pluralistic character of society

There is what constitutes the test of a living church. Are the teachings of your church consistent with the best in Scripture and Christian revelation? Is there a consistent meaningful bible study convening during the course of the lectionary year? Does your church gather for corporate intercessory prayer frequently? Are your church's priorities in order? Is the church impacting and transforming the immediate community where it resides? The world is now spoken of as a global village because of the increasingly pluralistic character of society. Does your church think globally, but act locally? If it is "His" church in construction, we are under obligation to follow blueprints of the Kingdom.

That Jesus came preaching the Kingdom is a fact of profound significance for the church. The Kingdom is such a key theme of Scripture that Howard Snyder says, *"it is a key thread in Scripture, tying the whole Bible together,"*[2] while Richard Lovelace admits, *"the messianic Kingdom is not only the main theme of Jesus' preaching; it is the central category unifying biblical revelation."*[3] The concept of the Kingdom of God *"not only involves in a real sense the total message of the Bible, it is to be found, in one form or another, through the length and breadth of the Bible,"* according to John Bright whose definitive work on The Kingdom of God continues to stand.[4] E. Stanley Jones was obsessed with the notion that Jesus' message was in fact that of *"the Kingdom of God".*[5] When we use the term Kingdom of God, it refers to the reign of God's sovereign order manifested on earth.

The church is spoken of as God's house (*oikos*), in Hebrews 3:1-6 in a metaphorical sense, but it is not the Kingdom. A review of the average church annual budget will reveal that eighty five percent is spent on its on self-aggrandizing agenda which often reveals a strange and offensive kind of spiritual narcissism. The church's alliance with success symbols of wealth and prosperity as its primary agenda short circuits its mandate to be free for the Kingdom. Any preoccupation with ancillary peripheral concerns will abort the church's faith that everything we do ought to be on behalf of God's Kingdom.

The primary focal point and goal of Evangelism is not to play numbers crunching statistical games, but to lead people into the Kingdom and worship the King. Howard Snyder, more than anyone I have read recently admonishes us of the confusion we encounter should we confuse church business with Kingdom business. According to Snyder, *"the church gets in trouble whenever it thinks it is in the church business rather than the Kingdom business.....church people think about how to get people into the church; Kingdom people think about how to get the church into the world. Church people worry that the world might change the church; Kingdom people work to see the church change the world.*[6] The church that promotes and works for Justice in the earth is working to expand the influence of the Kingdom of God.

To pray, *"thy Kingdom come, thy will be done in earth as it is in heaven"* is to participate in a revolutionary act. We seldom ask, how must it be in Heaven? I am compelled to believe that perpetual worship is taking place in Heaven. I am compelled to believe that there is unity in Heaven. There is also compelling evidence that missions of service are constantly performed by angelic couriers. That is why the church must be faithful and committed to its Kingdom oriented task as it lives between the *"present/and not yet"* tension of the demands of the Kingdom. It is the prophetic imagery of God's new order that keeps us encouraged during difficult times.

We are seriously in need of a theology of church development. Our theology will dictate our missiological imperatives. The principle of homogeneity (people gravitate toward their kind of people), may appear to be sociologically tenable, but is theologically unsound as a viable goal. The concept of globalism must be addressed if the church is to participate in Kingdom expansion on earth. His Kingdom on earth, should reflect the Kingdom of Heaven.

Homogeneity should be an explanation and description of a sociological phenomenon, but should not be embraced as a Kingdom ideal. The apocalyptic vision of the book of Revelation sees throngs and multitudes from every tribe, tongue and nation, before the throne of God. When the church allows the Kingdom to rule *"in earth as it is in heaven,"* it will invariably emerge as a victorious servant church ready to do God's bidding, all on behalf of the Kingdom that has no end.

Cultivating the Marriage Between Pastor and People

While meaningful church expansion involves prayer planning and smarter work, another essential component is necessary. Both pastor and congregation must have the desire to expand. Attitudes shape desires, and desires are determinative of the future shape of ministry. If you are saying, I want to expand, grow and maximize my potential, but your congregation is saying, "we do not want to expand." Guess what? You will not budge you will be the same size next year as you are this year, and perhaps smaller.

What is required for a fruitful marriage is a healthy relationship between the Pastoral leader and congregation

Similarly, if your flock is saying, we want to expand, grow and maximize our potential, but you are saying, *"I want to simply maintain what we currently have."* You will have what you desire!

If a Pastor does not desire to expand in ministry, one will develop a passive church by the process of "maintenance." A passive church does just enough to pay the bills, visit a few churches, maintain the status quo and merely get by. Passivity is an external sign of inward decay. A passive church holds fast to traditionalism and lives for the most part in the past.

What is required for a fruitful marriage is a healthy marital relationship between the Pastoral leader and congregation.

If marriages are made in heaven, they are consummated on earth. Marriages usually begin with a honeymoon, the period set aside for initial adjustment between newly weds. For a new pastorate, time is needed to build trust between pastor and people. The honeymoon should be over within a three year period. Short-range and long-range goals should be projected. It is the early season of church marriage, the relationship is in its infancy. New born babes in Christ are being nurtured, discipled for the larger task of ministry ahead.

A good marriage is not without its problems, but can be held together by virtue of its nature of being. It is an ontological reality. The two are linked by virtue of their being. Such a bonding is good for the relationship and give its stability in the face of the onslaught of pressure. Storms of disagreement can arise suddenly within the best of marriages. It is the anchoring function of an ontic marriage that keeps a relationship stable during the worst of times. A healthy marriage between pastor and people is not without its problems, but can be sustained and undergirded by cultivating respect and trust.

When a church has a healthy growing, nurturing relationship between pastor and people, visitors can feel it in the air. I know of a church in serious conflict between leader and factions, and it has taken its toll. Newcomers can sense the tension in the air as the pastor preaches defensive, fighting messages. It is a conflict where no one is yielding any ground. Conflict can be managed in creative ways so that the church's purpose for being is not defeated and reproach avoided at all cost.

During my first pastorate in Pennsylvania, I was placed in a warm friendly church on Philadelphia's Mainline. To this day I have several friends and cherish fond memories of that pastorate. I went through the challenges of being a single pastor, first year seminary student. My board of trustees consisted of persons who were firmly committed and dedicated to a single purpose. The first two years consisted primarily of preaching and maintenance. Few new ideas were birthed. I vividly recall the day the honeymoon was over.

We had our up times and down times, days of triumphs and days of disagreements. I had learned well from my mentor in ministry, Bishop O.T. Jones Jr., a few things that enabled me to cope with severe challenges. We had a fundamental agreement rooted in integrity that we were never to surprise each other in basic ministry relationships. No one was to spring surprises in board meetings or any other aspect of the church life. Under the leadership of my board chairman, Roland Williams, a person I respect to this day, we made it happen even during periods of flux, because we had a solid ontological marital relationship. I occasionally encounter Nathaniel and Ruth Goodson, Sr., Ike and Betty Jackson , Rev. Gordon and Debbie Bronner, Harold and Tony Thompson and the finest couple I know Harold and Lillie Miller in my visits to the area. We never tire of talking about the unique spiritual bond we had during some trying times.

There are few things as good as a healthy church marriage between pastor and people. A good marriage requires giving and receiving. A good marriage means either party is willing to admit fault. A good church marriage honors the spirit of the law rather than the letter of the law. Both parties realize that one does not have to be "right" at any cost. Like the parable of the prodigals, it is far better to be right in spirit and wrong in deed, than to be wrong in spirit, and right in deeds. Whatever I have achieved during this stage of ministry was initiated during my formative years of pastoral ministry at Memorial Church of God In Christ, Haverford, Pennsylvania..

One does not always have to be right at all costs. it is far better to be right in spirit and wrong in deed, than to be wrong in spirit, and right in deeds. A Good marriage means either party is willing to admit fault

In a marriage, an emotional divorce takes place long before formal divorce proceedings begin. Either or both of the parties begin to emotionally drift from the other. It is almost always the presence of a third factor that leads to an emotional divorce. An affair is present when either party becomes drawn toward something other than one's spouse to the point that it prevents the marriage from being consummated. People have affairs with money, toys, themselves as well as a third party. I have observed great ministries brought down because of the egomania of the pastor or trustees. When the things we get caught up in prevent us from fulfilling our primary duties to our partners, we are in for a parting of the ways. Most church fights are vicious and need not be so. As a pastor sensitive to the leading of the Holy Spirit, one will know when it is time to say goodbye. Let it be an amicable separation and departure if need be.

A healthy marriage is characterized by trust and communication. Communicate we must. A readily apparent sign of an unhealthy marriage on the verge of a final break-up is loss of communication. When a marriage is so bad, couples communicate by notes trouble is imminent. Communication takes place both directly and indirectly, by body language as well as speech. Mediation of disputes between pastor and people are usually difficult.

Religion is bound up with our emotions, and anything that threatens us at the deepest level of our beings, warrants some kind of defense. We build walls, fences by non-communication. Silence for some people means disapproval, rejection and denotes alienation. May the Holy Spirit rebuke the walls, fences and barriers we have erected between our brothers and sisters in Christ. May we be open to the fruits of reconciliation that only the children of the King can enjoy. We are called to be agents of reconciliation in a world torn by strife and discord. God expects us to model the mandates of the Kingdom as we consummate our relationships before Him.

When a pastor and congregation reaches mutual consensus to expand the ministry, it will happen. The harvests will bring forth and yield fruits of righteousness. When the consensus takes place, the Holy Spirit will be fully made manifest in His church. Our faith is that morning is breaking, and a new day is dawning for ministry as we recover the loss of integrity by living out the mandates of the Kingdom.

When the Death of A Church Means Life

To take Jesus serious and to radically follow Him is to follow Kingdom mandates. In order for the church to take serious such a challenge, something radical must take place. The "church of the people" must die in order for the church of the Kingdom to be born. In strange ways, God brings us to pivotal decisions at the crossroads of our lives. Toward the end of my last pastorate, I stood to preach and the leading was to challenge the congregation to become a church of the Kingdom. The price was too high for several members who eventually made their exit. The result was similar to an army slogan as we developed a "lean mean fighting machine" all on behalf of the Kingdom.

The caterpillar must diminish in order to release the butterfly. *"Except a corn of wheat fall into the ground and die it abideth alone, but if it die, it bringeth forth much fruit"* (John 12:24). The words of the Master teacher further reaffirms the principle that death precedes birth. We see it in nature as the icy grip of winter seizes the earth often laying waste vegetation. In nature it lies dormant as it awaits a budding springtime. Perhaps that is what the resurrection is really about..... the principle that death precedes birth.

The church in the world is in trouble because of its misplaced agenda. We are guilty of majoring in the minors and minoring in the majors. William Temple once remarked that *"the modern world reminded him of a department store where someone crept in over night and switched the price tag. They placed expensive tags on cheap items and inexpensive tags on items of high value."* Submission to authority is a continuing concern within the church. There is safety in authority. When leaders abuse their authority through misuse, the church gets in deeper trouble. When members are not submissive to positive leadership, the church gets in crisis.

We should not seek to denigrate people who resist our leadership. As we ascertain the reasons for their behavior, we must remember that there may be persons under our ministry who are by deeds asking for more room to grow elsewhere. If it is their decision, it may very well be a part of the principle at work, that death precedes life.

Get ready for a resurrection in your church, it CAN BE YOURS!

When Nibbles Becomes Bites....Only in Fishing

Somewhere I read fishing *"is the art of the wrist with a twist."* I make no pretense to being a fisherman. In fact this became clear a few decades ago when I was invited to go fishing one warm summer morning while visiting friends in Melbourne, Florida. I was given the proper equipment for fishing but little or no instructions about how to fish. For several hours I stood on the bridge spanning the intracoastal waterway beside a woman who was constantly catching fish. She gently smiled as she saw me fishing for nought. Finally, she gave me a few pointers covering everything from casting to handling a nibble. She had watched me yank the line too soon at the least hint of a bite.

Fish are vertebrate or backboned animals living mostly in water, respiring or obtaining oxygen for life processes by means of gills and/or lungs. Fish can be found in nearly every available aquatic habitat. They can be found in warmest springs and the coldest seas, in tropical oceans, mountain lakes and streams. Some live in the open seas, away from land, others are found in the lowest depths of the ocean in vast darkness. Some hide among stones, while others inhabit algae, weeds and rock crevices. Some are strictly nocturnal (night) while most hunt by day. Few bodies of water are without fish. Fish are the most numerous vertebrate animals known to humankind. There are known to be about forty thousand different kinds. Fish are highly variable in structure and adaptation. They walk, swim, and glide; some can see in the water and in the air. They can make many kinds of sounds; can produce light and even electricity. Each structure has its purpose for defense, food getting, and reproduction. [7]

It is this creature that prompted someone to say that fishing is *"an idle sport that makes persons and truth strangers." "An incessant expectation, and perpetual disappointment"- anonymous.* Fishing is an act of faith. A fisher is a person who is very dependent, and needs to be trustful..... There is an art in [fishing], from the mending of the net right on to the pulling it to shore. Charles Haddon Spurgeon has avidly stated, *"when Jesus Christ says, "follow me, and I will make you fishers of men," He means that you shall really catch men, that you really shall save some; for he that never did get any fish is not a fisherman.*[8] When Jesus Christ beckons us by his grace to follow Him, we must remember, only He can give us the best pointers on landing fish.

In Matthew 4:17ff, Jesus began to preach and to say, Repent, for the Kingdom of Heaven is at hand. In verse 18, Jesus sees Simon Peter and Andrew, [vs. 21]. Jesus the son of Zebedee and John his brother, and challenges them in verse 19. "And he saith unto them, follow me, and I will make you fishers of men." An invitation is given to peasant fisherman not to stop fishing, but to change your reasons. These were rough peasant fishermen who knew what it was to cast out a net and catch nothing in return. They knew failure as well as success. Ilka Chase, said, "the only people who never fail are those who never try." Thomas Edison's success as an inventor prompted him to say, "show me a thoroughly satisfied man and I will show you a failure." God alone fully knows what goes into the making of soul winner. If we come under His discipline, He will make us fishers of humankind.

The moment I took serious the informal lessons on the "art of twist of the wrist," I started catching fish. In the New Testament, the gospel was not a sermonic homily delivered from a platform, it was a life-style, a way of life inseparable from the proclaimer. It constituted the warp and woof of those who took Jesus seriously. In the New Testament "gospel" and "evangel" are both used to translate the same Greek word, *euaggelion*, which literally means *"good news."*

We live in a society where even the gospel has been made to be compatible with the "American Dream." We have concocted a cultural Christ who has all the trinkets and toys that constitutes the American success symbol. Culture is the pattern of meaning and values that a society utilizes to understand and evaluate itself. History, beliefs, traditions, mores constitutes the making of a culture. What does it mean to lead a person to Jesus Christ in an increasingly pagan culture? A society that protects pregnant lobsters and eagles by legal sanctions, but allows the murder of preborn children under the guise of right to privacy gobblygook. A society that reduces Christ to a patriotic symbol of Americanism cast in civic god diatribe. We replaced the Bible with condoms and metal detectors in our schools. We are in a serious moral crisis.

I choose to remain Christian because God wants to change our societal landscape, and we should desire to be a part of His activity. God is shaking the foundations of this decadent society. My analysis is not a pessimistic sourgraping complaint, the stage is set for authentic life transforming witnessing. Fish are ready for feeding. Teeming multitudes are starved for meaning, purpose and direction as the plot thickens.

The ancient *"euanggelion"* is still good news, bad news and indifferent news, but it is news from a far county. What are the odds of our success in leading one person to Jesus Christ. Let's consider gold mining for a perspective. We perhaps agree that one soul is infinitely more important than gold. But even mining is not done at random. They select a place using the best of technology. We are told that miners sift through 14,000 pounds of ore to get one ounce of gold. Or they sift through 224,000 ounces of ore to get one ounce of gold.

Fish are everywhere...Your outreach team must be willing to develop the skill of turning a nibble into a bite

What church would be willing to contact 224,000 possible prospects to get one person to confess Jesus as Lord.[9] Dr. D. James Kennedy has written an excellent training manual for outreach teams, entitled, ***Evangelism Explosion***, that will enable you to turn a nibble into a bite. Fish are everywhere. The lakes, streams and tributaries are brimming with fish. Your outreach team need to develop the skill of turning a nibble into a bite.

Do not send untrained undisciplined people out to do personal witnessing. Should they say the wrong thing as they carry your church name, the fallout could be embarrassing. Train your outreach team. Expose them to cross-cultural training if possible, but training should not be an option. Fish should really be given a chance to fully engage the bait. When we would use fishing corks, once the cork went under, we knew we had a good bite. In making our Christian witness we must never begin scaling fish before they have been landed.

The worst thing we can do with an unbeliever is to begin the process of indoctrination before salvation. It is tantamount to being on the outside looking in. We have to earn the right to share this special news from the King. We share in *charis* [grace] in *doxa* [glory to God]; in *eulogia* [blessing]; in *diakonia* [service]; all expressive of *koinonia* [love in community]. The Gospel we proclaim embraces the whole of the cosmos, as God works out His redemptive purposes in the world.

UPGRADE YOUR EQUIPMENT!

Even fishing as a sport has changed. Gone are the bamboo poles that would break under mild pressure. The use of a cork has become a thing of the past. The fishing rod appears to be in. The kind of bait one uses has to do with the kind of fish sought. We spent many hours searching for worms to be used as bait. Today bait-casting lures work as effective as live bait.

Two and one half decades after the advent of the "Jesus People" movement in North America the religious landscape has changed. The social, political and spiritual climate that spanned the formation of Chuck Smith's Calvary Chapel in Costa Mesa California, and the late John Wimber's Vineyard Church Movement has changed. We have lived through several serious religious scandals that rocked the foundation of many Christian prospects. Cynicism - the belief that self-interest is the motive of all human conduct, appears to be gaining strength when its comes to the church in North America, all characterized by a new form of greed..

Integrity and credibility heads the list in most discussions about the influence of religion in our times. It means we must change the bait and upgrade our equipment by becoming creative. It means exploring new forms of ministry. It means living on the cutting edge of where God is and participating in what God is doing. It means leaving our cozy comfort zones so we can respond to the Lord of the church in radical obedience. It means acquiring the courage to engage in risk-taking on behalf of the Kingdom. It means a re-reading and re-interpretation of Acts 20:20, often referred to as the 20:20 vision of the church. The whole of Asia Minor was evangelized within a two year period without the use of mass media as they went from house to house.

Steve Sjogren, pastor of the Vineyard Christian Fellowship in Cincinnati has begun modeling what he labels servant evangelism... 'befriending Jesus" friends who are experiencing pain by sharing deeds of kindness and service. By developing more than 40 creative outreaches ranging from free car washes to free cleaning of house/apartments, Sjogren skyrocketed from 35 people to 1,600 within a six year period.

His ministry operates on a simple premise often referred to as a conspiracy of kindness: *that God is passionately in love with unbelievers and can win them most effectively through acts of kindness."* The free deed of *diakonia* [service] open the door for making a point through the back door entrance of those who were the recipients of free service. They merely changed the bait, upgraded the equipment and are currently making their impact. The byline made a telling point, *"a rake, a prayer and a servant's heart may be all it takes to win the lost with God's love."*[10]

In fishing equipment, methods and technique are all very important. While sport fishing has become prominent, still-fishing is the most common and simplest form of fishing. In still-fishing, the hook is usually baited with live bait and the line is left resting stationary in the water. With this method, the fisher does not actively seek fish by frequent casts. The fisher waits for the fish to find the bait. Most fish can be caught with still-fishing methods. Whether you are fly casting straight casting, bait casting or tournament casting, equipment is important. The line is the most important item for every caster. Once the bait-casting lures [spoons, spinners and plugs] are attached to the line, you are ready for action. People are ready available and waiting, but our lines must be upgraded.

For Dialogue and Reflection

1. Is there a fundamental difference between church work and Kingdom work? Church people and Kingdom People?

2. If the primary task of theology is to clarify the nature of the Christian faith within the believing Community, is theology important?

3. What can you do to facilitate the marriage between pastor and people?

4. In what ways can triviality thwart the work of the Kingdom in the church?

Chapter
5 Liberate and Reclaim Your City

The Source of Inner City Misery

While I make no claims to being a bona fide urban missionary or a licensed evangelist, which is really where my heart is and where God can most readily be envisioned today, God's footprints are readily visible in inner cities throughout the world. He is often found in the places where the pain is almost unbearable and the suffering deplorable. Listening to God's footsteps requires enormous discipline, especially for people who are skilled in speaking and are accustomed to having others listen. Listening to God takes place within a set of commitments. Listening to God for the sake of discernment entails listening for the throbbing pain, the insecurities, the fears and the hopelessness that offers clues to the anxiety and alienation present in our society.

If we are alienated for any reason from the inner city, we are ipso facto alienated from God.

Since the decline of Communism in Eastern block nations and the fall of the Berlin Wall, there has been a strong resurgence of missionary zeal to missionize the Soviet Union and other nations in the region. Initially I was moved with deep sentiment as I saw many youthful mission teams rush to battle That task is important as a breakthrough we have all longed for in view of the long history of totalitarian rule in communist controlled nations. God forbid that we forget the domestic challenges at our doorstep. A few years ago, someone in jest in attempting to describe several key cities in morbid pathological language, made an announcement. New York City had a heart attack, Los Angeles a debilitating stroke, Chicago, terminal cancer, Houston, on long term dialysis as a result of renal failure. Satire often lifts up the real depth of the human situation and like myth plumbs such depth for meaning. Is the Lord of the city saying to us, physician, heal thyself?

The most difficult of all cures to effect, is that of self-healing. The first major hurdle is that of denial. How often we have heard people near the verge of collapse, later admit, "I never realized I was that ill." I asked a close relative recently, when was your last physical? The response was not since I left the military over thirty years ago. He has been victimized by the fear of the unknown. In his mind, the less he knows the better off he could function. He is being controlled by the power of "what might be." The last thing we want to risk is the uncomfortable notion of healing ourselves. Once the disease has been diagnosed, how are we to effect the care? How may we verify the cure?

Physician, heal thyself, because you hold the key to healing medicine in the midst of a hostile bacteria filled environment.. Physician heal thyself because you have been imbued with knowledge of the scientific approach to treating various diseases. Physician, heal thyself, because your range of knowledge far outdistanced the average person when it comes to diagnosis and understanding prognosis [assessment of the probable course of a disease]. Physician, heal thyself because you can write prescriptions to remedy all kinds of diseases. Does a physician have the objectivity to cure oneself? Is there a balm in Gilead to heal the sin sick soul? If so, physician heal thyself.

The missiological paradigm is shifting. Africans for example are now coming to our shores in order to evangelize North America. In and around the nation's capitol several Ghanian churches have sprouted. I have initiated conversation with some of these fine pastors. Their sincerety and commitment is unmatched. Their worship services are filled with awe and reverence. They represent significant signs of hope for the renewal of the church in America. The tables are being turned, the house is being renovated, the furniture is being re-arranged, the last shall be first and there is very little we can do about it. God is "doing a new thing in the earth." Some of the finest proclamation we know today is beginning to take place within developing nations on the continents of Africa and South America. Could it be that the persistent life of cultural poverty has made these persons far more sensitive to the living bread which came down from above?

Healing, in many instances is a process. A specialist in Internal medicine and personal friend Dr. Samuel Hunter once disclosed to me that his task was to first find the locus of the disease eliminate the cause either through medication or surgery. That, anyone taking medicine should always follow carefully the instructions written up by the pharmacy. His point was, medicine is precise. They know the rate that bacteria left untreated can multiply within the human body. The health status of our inner cities is in the high risk category. Because our cities are at risk, the Lord of the city and of the world is beckoning us to seek the welfare, the *"shalom"*(peace) of the city. The Lord of the church once wept over Jerusalem as he foresaw its coming destruction. He did not shed a few tears, he wept bitterly. While these are not the best of times for our inner cities, it is the best of times for the church. The Incarnate God cannot be bound up in some seminary text as mere theological theory, He must become in-fleshed in the blood, guts and tissues of society. The Master physician wants those physicians who work under His supervision to heal themselves.

It is not my attempt, to generate an anti-missionary movement. It is difficult to envision persons who have little or no experience in combat zones to be airlifted and parachuted into raging combat without proper training. Did not Henri Nouwen come close to this reality in his challenging book, **The Wounded Healer?** The experience of living with a serious, gaping, deep wound prepares us to become sensitive healers! Living with a wound deepens our compassion and increases greater sensitivity toward others. Pain is one of the most sincere messengers that the Creator incorporated into our autonomic system. It is withstanding the threshold of pain that determines the kind of physician we will become. Physician, come back to the inner city and heal thyself!

The period of the Great Migrations, 1930 to 1970 contributed to massive movements of African-Americans from the deep South to the Mid-West and Northern sections of the United States. During this time frame, the process of suburbanization began just after World War II when U.S. veterans began purchasing housing and land in what we call the suburbs. This trend gained momentum during the sixties and seventies as corporations such as Shell Oil Company moved westward across Philadelphia's City line Avenue into a neighboring suburbs as a cost-saving venture. Such a move left a gaping hole in the city's shrinking revenue tax-base. Other corporations moved further South to sun-belt cities such as Atlanta, Georgia, or West to places such as Garden City, California. Those who remain in the city must pay higher taxes to replace such revenue. Suburbanites no longer need to go to central city for shopping or jobs, when all they need to do is drive a few blocks to high-tech manufacturing centers with sprawling industrial office parks and gleaming malls. Professional sports arenas, art museums, music halls have all joined the exodus to suburbia. So did the churches.

SUBURBANIZATION

From 1950 to 1980, according to U.S. News and World Report, the population of suburbia nearly tripled, from 35.2 million to 101.5 million - about 45 percent of the nation's total population. During the same period, central cities grow only modestly, from about 50 million to 68 million, or 30 percent of total U.S. population. During this period, many Northern cities lost hundreds of thousands of people. Today one half of America's 250 million people live in suburbia in contrast to only one quarter of a million in the central cities.

Suburbia and urbia (inner city) are two nations separated by class and commute time on the freeways

The economic impact of such a transition has been disastrous for remaining city dwellers. Our cities have been severely undermined with city dwellers having to absorb the losses. From 1987 to 1997 major flight to surburbia from cities like New York, Philadelphia, Washington, Boston has taken place with great rapidity placing further economic pressure on the urban icon. Parallel to this trend is the return to the inner cities for those who can afford the upper priced high rise.

Suburbia and urbia, are two nations separated by class race and driving time on the freeways. In most major cities the reality is the same, suburbia dictates and continues to dominate the course of economic and social life on the landscape of North America as we enter the Twenty First Century.

DETERIORATING INFRASTRUCTURES

The growth and viability of a city is dependent on the strength of its physical infrastructure, i.e. its source of energy/power, water distribution, sewage system, bridges and network of roads. In New York city, as in other major urban cities, water is a precious commodity. Supplying the city with 250 million gallons of water a day is the Catskill system built in 1917. Through an ingenious siphon constructed under the Hudson River, water flows through some 6,000 miles of water mains buried under city streets. In Manhattan alone, over 120 miles of water mains installed prior to 1870.

When breaks occur in these lines they need to be replaced. As the physical infrastructure ages, problems of major proportions increase. The cost of replacement is left at the doorstep of a shrinking population. Without Federal assistance it is highly unlikely that such infrastructures will remain viable. Add to this the maintenance of 65 bridges and 12 tunnels that keep the island of New York linked to the rest of the continent.[1] Perhaps that is why "Imagineers" are needed to keep urban areas such as New York viable as they plan the metropolis of tomorrow.

Those who escaped to the suburbs did not leave all the problems behind. The misery of urbia in such challenges as increasing crime waves has spread to the fringes of the suburbs. Many of the challenges ignored by most people who thought they were largely confined to the ghetto is now at suburban doorsteps. A cellular phone and two guns appears to be the solution for people who never thought of it. In the words of the Prophet Amos, *"It will be as though a man fled from a lion only to meet a bear, as though he entered his house and rested his hand on the wall only to have a snake bite him."* [Amos 5:19,]. In today's climate there are no safe havens. Crime has no respect for geographic, ethnic, class location, it is a crises of significant proportions and is a sign of the times.

INADEQUATE HOUSING

Over crowdedness invariably appears to be a key feature of inner city life. Laboratory experiments in experimental psychology indicates that when certain animals are confined to an overpopulated space, they kill each other. It is believed that human beings similarly become extremely more aggressive when placed in close quarters. The four largest cities in the U.S. stand with teeming populations of diverse peoples. In the last thirty years the greatest migration in human history has occurred. Some one billion people have moved from rural poverty to the mega-city slums squatter area. These migrant poor now make up 40% of the world's cities and their numbers double every ten years. By the year 2,000 it is predicted that there will be 40 mega-cities of 5 to 25 million, 2,000 A.D., most with 508 to 1,000 squatter areas. And 400 cities over one million, each with 100 poor areas.[2]

Neighborhoods are diminished by the use of unethical practices of blockbusting by Realtors and redlining by banking institutions. Land and quality housing are at an absolute premium in most inner cities, leaving deteriorating housing as the only option for the poor who often pay premium rent to greedy landlords. Lack of ownership by the poor further contributes to the problem of decay within the inner city.

DRUGS: THE SCOURGE OF OUR TIME

Even crimes that do not pass a cost-benefit test may seem worth attempting to a drug user for money. Money is the major motivation for most substance abusers. The prison population in the U.S. has doubled over the past decade as part of a "get tough" on crime policy, but that has not solved the problem of the proliferation of drug trafficking. More states are building larger prisons and jails as a panacea for rising crime. Unfortunately our criminal justice system is a poor excuse for rehabilitation Former New York City Police Commissioner and National Drug Czar, Lee Brown, once said *"The sad truth is that while we've ended the war in the Gulf, we still have to fight on the streets of our city."*

It is difficult to instruct a youth in Washington D.C. or Los Angeles to seek employment at a burger joint and report to school when that youngster as a small-time street dealer grosses an average of $48,000 a year. They net $24,000 tax-free after paying for the drugs and their runners. This nation spends $60 billion a year on all aspects of law enforcement and yet crime and substance abuse escalates. The underground drug economy underwrites and subsidizes the present economy. The threat of the loss of our youth is so severe, some people just simply give up. No where is the drug problem so severe as in the inner city. What is financed in the suites, more than often end up on the streets.

When churches and neighborhood associations link up and pressure local neighborhood markets to stop selling gang and drug paraphernalia, it will make a difference. The concept of community policing in Miami, Los Angeles and several metro cities is effective. In Miami the Metro-Dade force teamed with community residents to take back a crime-ridden area. Such

Police officers can be aggressive without being abusive as they encounter residents of the inner city

teamwork resulted in 5,257 arrest, $1.7 million in drugs and currency seized, 316 firearms confiscated and 40 crack houses demolished-all without one complaint of excessive force [see U.S. News and World Report, May 11, 1992]. Violent crimes dropped between 19 and 46 percent within a year proving that police can be aggressive without being abusive in working with residents of urbia.

In the nooks and crannies of the "Hood," far removed from media reporters and newspaper coverage, some residents in South Central Los Angeles knew that their city had the distinction of having more liquor stores than the combined states of Rhode Island and Pennsylvania. It took a riot to reduce them to rubbish. That was a tough loss for new enterprising business entrepreneurs who recently arrived from the Orient. Drugs dope and alcohol are the medicine of slaves. You can be sure God is judging and purging the city. Martin Luther King Jr. addressed violence in a few words; *"a riot is the language of the unheard."*

POLICE INSENSITIVITY

The predicate for change in the way police in the inner city respond to citizens in the nineties is the Rodney King incident. Rodney King emerged as a mythic symbol of justice denied in the courts. For more than a year the world court of opinion watched the most endlessly replayed videotape ever made. The world watched a writhing body of an African-American male twisting on the ground under kicks and nightstick blows from Euro-American male officers of the Los Angeles police department. Prosecutors thought the video tape showing Rodney King clubbed and kicked 56 times in 81 seconds would guarantee a conviction. Instead this "in your face " tape provided a reason for the jury to find four policeman not guilty. For the prosecution it seemed like an open-and shut case. For forty eight hours, Los Angeles became an urban holocaust as hatred and resentment ruled the streets. Once again, the besieged African-American community suffered the most. It was by no means coincidental that nearly all the major ghetto riots since the 1960's have been sparked by some incident involving an arrest of African-Americans by Anglo cops. To many African-Americans police brutality is an ever present threat to their very existence.

A part, of every humane American irregardless of ethnic origins took a beating with Rodney King. March 3, 1991, will be etched in the collective conscience of America whether we agreed with the verdict or not

One month after the class riot occurred I co-incidentally encountered three young African-Americans selling T-shirts inscribed with the words "Justice for L.A. Four." One of the young men was the brother of Damien "Football" Williams one of the four people tried in the near fatal beating of the L.A. truck driver Reginald Denny during the riot. He indicated that police were called to check on a complaint by an Asian driver whose window was struck by a seventeen year old youth. The police apprehended the young man and proceeded to beat him, his mother and several women challenged them. When the police started placing choke-holds and head-locks on African-American females, young brothers entered the fray in hand-to-hand combat. After several minutes of struggle, police were ordered to leave the area. As soon as they departed the vicinity of Florence and Normandie, the riot broke out covering a 46 square mile area of South Central Los Angeles.

That conversation helped me face the stark reality that most of us are not willing to face. The rest of urban America is not far removed from the class riot that has so grotesquely re-arranged the landscape of Los Angeles. Since ethnics living in the inner city have far more than police brutality to demonstrate concern about. Encountering high unemployment, drug pushers and criminals, widespread poverty, inadequate housing, and survival, they too understand the seriousness of one incident.

It only takes the spark of one seriously flawed, media-enlarged incident to set an urban holocaust blazing. Eleven years before I accepted a pastorate in Los Angeles, Watts erupted, precipitated by police insensitivity. Before the fires were quenched thirty-four people lay dead. In many blighted urban communities where poverty and crime is dominant, people often experience helplessness which becomes resentment and anger, such anger, is then vented upon an increasing variety of ethnic cultures that live in close proximity.

Add to this are roaming volatile youth gangs who have at their disposal massive arsenals of firepower, combined with this are the bleak prospects for economic woes. Major industries such as Goodyear, Firestone, Bethlehem Steel, General Motors, Hughes Aircraft, Lockheed and other employers have either down-sized or closed down their regional operations. Declines in the construction and finance industries has exacerbated the problem.

Where Have the Real Teachers Gone?...The Urban Classroom

Fresh out of seminary in the mid-sixties, my first real job in the private sector was that of a coordinator of the Neighborhood Youth Corps project under the sponsorship of the Philadelphia Health and Welfare Council. It was a part of President Lyndon Baines Johnson War On Poverty. My task was to find High School drop-outs, employ them with cooperating agencies in the Philadelphia metro area and provide supportive counseling. It was my first primary encounter with gang members from North and South Philadelphia. I was pastoring a suburban church and working in the inner city simultaneously. We had a model project. We had some losses, but we also had some success stories that made a difference. We were educated to some extent by the kids from the "hood." We learned that "two dongs and a split" in gang ghettoese meant, "leaving at two-thirty." We encountered some bright academics who merely needed a role model they could identify with and revere.

It is not uncommon to find High School students in inner city schools who simply cannot read beyond fifth grade level. High density classrooms are usually the norm rather then the exception. Overcrowdedness at home and school can have disastrous effects upon young minds. Poor facilities and academic materials such as hand-me-down textbooks run counter to a basic education. Bureaucratic red tape interferes with strong implementation of educational imperatives. Many teachers are simply disciplinarians, who are merely holding on for life. The drop-out rate continues to plague inner city youth. When non-academic problems are the norm, very little teaching can occur. Urban-education experts cite poor nutrition, the stress of living in a violent environment combined with non-academic problems must be addressed more adequately, if inner-city students are to remain in school.

The U.S. Labor department reported that in 1991 unemployment areas 9 percent among High School graduates but 23 percent among dropouts. The report cites the good news in recent decades is that the dropout rate for African-Americans has fallen substantially. The bad news is that this rate remains excessively high in many inner-city districts.[3] That while the U.S. Education Department is spending $6.1 billion on behalf of disadvantaged students under its chapter 1 "compensatory education program, many leading educators find the program lacking."

A young graduate student recently shared his encounter with an urban school back east for incorrigibles who had been expelled from every school they had attended. He noticed all students wore expensive designer clothing and laughed him to scorn because he appeared in pony sneakers. Some students had cellular telephones and all of them had beepers. One drove up in a gold plated Mercedes, while another sat in class and counted thirty-five $100 bills. He threatened to discipline one student by the threat of expulsion, but was told by the principal that there was no where to go. Once the paycheck for these youngsters was held up in the bureaucratic red tape [they were being paid to attend class]. When the instructor entered the classroom, they had stacked desks all the way to the ceiling in playful protest. With a background in electrical engineering, he never got a chance to teach one single day. While this may not be the norm, it mirrors the kind of chaos prevalent in urban schools across this nation. We are in crisis because no one really knows who's in charge?

Institutional Racism....Demons With a New Address

To deny the all-pervasiveness and virulence of institutional racism in American society is to set one self up for disillusionment, failure and frustration in the long run. We were warned several decades ago by the Kerner Report that this nation was moving toward two separate societies, one black and the other white. Very few institutions heeded the warning including the church. Elsewhere I have written, "to take Jesus seriously is to become "offended" by Him. The Greek word used in the New Testament is *scandilizo*. It literally means to stumble or trip over something Jesus has said - derived from *"scandalon"* a trapping device. To become so disturbed by the Kingdom demand of Jesus that you are actually propelled toward greater faith. If we are not scandalized by the blatant manifestation of racism in ourselves and in the church - then perhaps we have never really understood Him.[4]

Dave Claerbaut, a Euro-American Urban missiologist sets forth a trenchant analysis of racism and asserts that this is not meant to be an indictment. However for many it is:

...For to be white and some what racist is normal. For just as a person who regularly breathes polluted city air should not be the least defensive about having some pollution in his lungs, so a person who is regularly exposed to a racist and prejudice-laden society could hardly be expected not to be somewhat prejudiced....If white racism is defined as having notions of white supremacy, it becomes rather easy to see how these tendencies become subconsciously internalized at a very early age. Thus these racist nations calcify. All agree that a person's environment is a major influence on his attitudes values, beliefs and behaviors. Thus a white pastor or urban worker is by conditioning and environment at least partly racist.[5]

Racism continue to be pervasive in American life on a day-to-day basis

Claerbaut cites four related and interacting historical and sociological factors that contribute to individual racism and prejudice. They are historical conditioning, cultural conditioning, psychological and social structure. Racism exists when one group intentionally or unintentionally refuses to share power and resources with another group. Racism exists when the group in power maintains dominance from a base or stance of power. Racism is prejudice linked with power. It is difficult and virtually impossible for African-Americans and/or powerless minorities to be racist. They may be prejudiced, which means to prejudge or make categorical generalizations about others without having the facts.

At its core, racism is a spiritual problem, idolatrous self-worship rooted in pride [hubris] and violates the First Commandment fueled by the twin gods of complacency and idolatry, it is a distortion of the Creator's grand "rainbow" design and a perversion of His intent that there should be variety among the races. God created persons of a different hue, His creatures invented race and racism. God willed that there should be variety among His children, and racism is a perversion of such variety. "Correlate racism takes place" writes Joseph Barndt in *Liberating Our White Ghetto*. *"When discrimination or other forms of minority exploitation occur as a by-product of policies or practices which in themselves are not racist. It may be a totally unintentional practice within an institution which is honestly seeking to be non-discriminatory."*[6]

The typical Euro-American response, is why should we be held liable for what our fore-parents did to slaves? It is tantamount to the reality that African-Americans bear in their person the scars of slavery even though they are 450 years removed from the reality of the physical incarceration and bondage of their fore-parents. The rapidity of urbanization forced a specific humanity into the urban ethos without challenging the ruralism brought to bear. To survive in urbia requires disbanding ruralism and adopting a social perspective, a frame of reference appropriate to urban life. This process can also become a form of dehumanization for persons who cannot make adjustment to same.

Institutional racism has changed its address, but not its being. It has to do with discrimination and racial superiority displayed, implemented and practiced in the day-to-day functions of societal institutions. A review of most institutions will find the demon of racism somehow, some way structured consciously and unconsciously into the warp and woof of institutional fabric. Like cancer it is pervasive. It comes home when you must explain to your nine year old why all the people behind the counter at the bank, post office, hospital, university and large corporations are Euro-American. That same child sees the maid, janitor and garbage collectors are people of color. For a child that is the beginning of the process of inferiority.

It really comes home when a Christian university has a Euro-American Administration faculty and staff. We see the same trends in theological seminaries who claim to be preparing students to spend the rest of their lives working with diversity. We see the manifestation of institutionalized racism in Christian publishing firms who have no minorities on staff and has not published any books by minorities, which subtly implies "black folk can't write" the same as "white men can't jump."

Institutional racism is prevalent in all places within the Christian sector. African-Americans and other minorities are used to underwrite the on-going functioning and presence of even Christian conferences and even old fashion camp meetings. Minorities can sing and occasionally read Scripture, but cannot participate in the corporate decision-making areas where the programs and players are decided upon. Christian conferences should reflect ethnic diversity. Unless you are a part of the traditional "good old boys" network you may never get a hearing, even though you have a message. Once you speak out on an issue such as racism you get black-balled, black-listed and labeled as a trouble maker. Why can't a person be "white-balled" and "white-listed"? We have been programmed to believe black is negative.

I spoke out against racism some two and a half decades ago at a booming charismatic renewal conference held in Pittsburgh, Pennsylvania and was never invited back. If they have not missed me, I have never missed them. Many anglo churches continue the practice of inviting "safe Negroes" to their pulpit and conferences and are silent all year long on the subject. The white church should lead the way in apologizing to African-Americans for slavery rather than defend the status quo. Prophets do not expect or treasure return engagements. God will open doors no human being dare not try to close. No weapon formed against you shall prosper. Vance Havener once said, *"there are three ways to silence a prophet, pressure, persecution and promotion."*

Pastor Frederick K. Price of the now well known Crenshaw Christian Center recently took on Kenneth Hagin, Jr., Tulsa, Oklahoma for his refusal to apologize for a public racist statement regarding African-Americans. After a white teen-ager was impregnated by a Black male in Hagin's congregation, pressure was brought to bear by white parents. Hagin made the mistake of trying to resolve it by publicly stating; "it is okay to socialize with Blacks, but not to marry them." Unfortunately Hagin stated what many white Christians honestly believe. Unfortunately a few Black pastors attempted to support Kenneth Hagin,Jr. Unfortunately, many Blacks continue to support such ministries. A pentecostal pastor in the Northern Virginia area recently stated that when whites get to heaven many of them will be shocked to find that there will be no differences. The problem is many whites see racism as a cultural aberration rather than sin.

In the May 8, 1998 edition of USA Today in an article by Tony Mauro, institutional racism was highlighted as the reason the Supreme Court in our nation has faulted on diversity. The article went on to point out that four of the nine justices, including Chief Justice William Rehnquist on the court since 1972, have never hired a Black law clerk. According to Randy Jones, President of the National Bar Association "there are qualified African-Americans.........Justices tend to engage in the practice of choosing clerks who look and think like them." Law clerks are responsible for screening cases that the court will consider and writing first drafts of opinions for Justices. Does this not make the highest court of the land suspect regarding some of the recent decisions it has made especially with regard to affirmative action.? God have mercy on the soul of Justice Clarence Thomas, a man who voted against the very affirmative action programs that undergirded his education.

The white church should lead the way in apologizing to African-Americans for slavery rather than defend the status quo

For Christians, racism is reverse stewardship. Racism is expensive to maintain. Property values decrease, police forces are expanded, tax appropriations are diverted to problem areas and businesses are destroyed as was demonstrated in the L.A. riots. Such persons are denied the opportunity of expressing their vocation in caring for and building community, and to that degree dehumanization is inevitable. In brief, "that is the tragedy of slavery in the United States and its continued expression in racism."[7] There are increasing numbers of African-Americans both Christian and non who have been coerced by their sense of history to believe that most Euro-Americans are racist until proven otherwise in order to retain their sanity. This argument is a sure defense mechanism against future disillusionment.

Political Primacy.........Achieving the Possible

Toward the end of the nineteenth century when the church in North America encountered rapid social change due to increased urbanization and technical industrialization, the Social Gospel under the leadership of Walter Rauschenbush, Washington Gladden with the thought of Shailer Matthews later coming to the fore. Even as the product of Protestant Liberalism, it sought to bring the Kingdom of God to bear on the social ills of that era. The fundamental critique by the conservatives was that they made a far too close identification of the Kingdom with the social order. Today a unifying point of contact is needed between the church and the inner city. In the era of advanced technics and shifting values, politics appears to be the most attractive and realistic option that the urban missioner must understand in order not to enter the urban arena empty.[8]

Aristotle the Greek philosopher defined politics as the *"art of achieving the possible."* With Aristotle in mind Paul Lehmann of Union Seminary, New York spoke of the political task as that of *"making and keeping human life truly human."* It is in the realm of ends that politics and the Christian faith are compatible. That is precisely what God is doing in Christ in the world, redeeming and restoring humankind to its full humanity. Indeed Jesus knew what it was to be fully and truly human. God continues to act in history giving meaning to human destiny. Since we live in an urban world, it is through the structures of community that we can participate with the Lord of the city.

We must be cautious not to imply that politics is the only institution that God is working through in urbia. Nor should we confuse politics as it is defined ideally with what passes for political reality in our time. God can use whatever means necessary to effect His will. God can employ Cyrus as His anointed and use the *"wrath of humankind"* to praise Him. Politics in its fundamental essence has to do with the task of making life more humane through organized means. This involves the correct use of power.

Through the sweep of biblical history the political perspective is present. Scripture is replete with political language and imagery, covenants, thrones, subjects, dominions, rulers, judges and finally one perceived to be the expected Messiah comes declaring the time has come to establish God's rule on earth. God chose to deal with His people through covenants. The Mosaic Covenant was significant as a point of reference for community cohesion. The community of Israel was bound by the terms of this political instrument known as a covenant. God does operate through the structure of human community.

A continuing concern from the Christian community is the question, to what extent should the church become involved in politics? A better question might be. to what extent are we already involved? Virtually every church building that occupies space with a city block is considered a political and economic entity subject to zoning laws, restrictions, ordinances and specific taxes. The taxes we pay, the votes we cast, the municipal services we request and receive, the health services and Social Security payments we contend for are all part of the political process. The political arena constitutes a major

Liberate and Reclaim Your City

factor in shaping our environment and world and should be rightfully addressed by believers who are concerned about transforming this society and making a decisive difference.

The fundamental question for the church should be what ought to be the nature of our response? In a political crisis, the cost of inaction is greater than the cost of action. The person who refuses to vote " for whatever reason " ends up casting a vote just the same. To those who argue for Christian non-involvement on the grounds that politics is corrupt misunderstands the fundamental nature of politics.

Politics is indemic to humankind and is as old as humankind itself. According to Aristotle by nature we are social and political animals. Our political institutions have extended power into every aspect of our lives. Many political scientists estimate that the scope and intensity of the Federal government alone has increased one hundred-fold since 1914. Our once cherished freedom of personal privacy has been invaded by computer memory banks and assigned numbers to the point that we almost feel violated. The issues we face will not only affect our future but the future of all civilizations. The point is that the bulk of the overwhelming mass of domestic and international problems confronting us requires responsible solutions and such solutions depend upon a valid decision-making process called politics.

Certain politicians maybe corrupt, but politics in and of itself is no more corrupt than economics. Because certain bankers embezzle funds does not make economics corrupt. It was the confessing church that played an important role in challenging Hitler as the antichrist in prewar Germany and figured prominently in the fall of the Berlin Wall. These were political challenges and actions for which we are all thankful today. It is in such a context that politics may be defined as purposeful action which involves the use of power for the accomplishment of certain ends.

Urban missioners dare not enter the inner city empty, but with renewed vigor and new visions for the city, for implementing ministry and to promote and effect spiritual well-being in our urban jungles. It will entail coming to grips with the decisive urgency and impact of public policy issues. We are called to be light in a dark world. We are urged by our Lord to be the salt of the earth, recalling that God is Lord of the universe and that includes the political arena. Indeed our urgent task is to "seek the welfare"of the cities in which we are exiled.

THE CHURCH IS.....WHAT IT DOES

Evangelization is inclusive of a total process whereby person's are led to embrace Jesus Christ as Savior and acknowledge Him as Lord. As followers of the Way we are called to be God's people in the world. God and the city are correlative terms in Scripture. God has always appeared in history joining the exploited and poor, acting against human injustice. The primary purpose of evangelization is to introduce salvation to those who are downtrodden, beaten down by life and who have no hope. Evangelization takes place once the church hears the cry of suffering humanity and sees the brokenness and violence in the nation's cities. Evangelization is to bring wholeness. Spiritual wholeness comes as a result of the acceptance of the message of proclamation. Proclamation leads to salvation and salvation points to liberation. The church is called to be the visible expression of Christ's dawning Kingdom.

For me Scripture is the guide, the blueprint, the map for all programs, policies and agendas that point toward liberation

While many definitions and approaches to liberation abound, the view espoused here has developed from a religio-cultural perspective forged out of my own religious experience. Liberation is freedom from the various bondages that would hinder us from maximizing our potential as we radically follow Jesus the Liberator. For me Scripture is the guide, the blueprint, the map for all programs, policies and agendas that point toward liberation. They must evolve from the nexus of basic religious experience, under the guidance of the revolutionary transforming presence of God as Holy Spirit. We are always liberated from something to something. Liberation does not occur in a vacuum. We are liberated from oppression. Oppression is intricately bound up with domination, and domination is as old as recorded history. Oppression of all forms must be encountered in God's name.

In the Exodus event we see God displaying His liberating power as He delivers His chosen people from bondage into freedom. The former Hebrew slaves are free as God brought His power to bear against the Pharaohs of that era. God chooses sides as He participates in the liberation of His people as He tears down the old established orders. "Out of Egypt have I called my son." In the Exodus event, salvation is intimately bound up with, tied to, and is an integral part of political liberation.

Any proclamation that fails to deal with the structures of oppression, racism, sexism, capitalism, etc. is to be viewed as a preservation of the status quo and therefore, opposed to liberation.

Proclamation set forth with a deep sense of mission and integrity invariably leads to salvation both at the personal and corporate levels of human existence. Such a Gospel will impact social institutions and systems toward wholeness.

The Gospel [eueggelion] of proclamation must of necessity shift its style to the victimized who are often trapped in the ghettos of the contemporary polis. They are often victimized by drugs, unemployment, social dysfunction, and whose very lives are intimately bound up in life and death issues of survival. It is to such persons that the Gospel is proclaimed in fullness, making sense out of life. The traditional and fundamental notion of redemption must be linked to the liberation of the oppressed, in order to accomplish a full-orbed faith and to achieve wholeness among those whose life-style is influenced, shaped, and in most instances determined by dehumanizing forces and structures operating within the confines of the contemporary polis. The concern of Jesus was *"when the Son of Man comes, will He find faith on the earth?"* [Luke 18:8]

When the Gospel of salvation-liberation is proclaimed those who receive it are liberated through a process of spiritual de-colonization from destructive values and idols which have held sway over the psychological domain of the society. Feeding the hungry means understanding micro and macro-economics and purging systems and structures of injustice and institutionalized evil. The Spirit is not an isolated portion of God. The Spirit is God and God is expressed in community shattering and renewing, rending, and healing, revealing and transforming, lifting and liberating a people unto Himself. When the human spirit is grasped and energized by the Holy Spirit, it is given the necessary power to go beyond our normally anticipated human ability and comprehension. For, "where the Spirit of the Lord is there is liberty."

It is my strong contention that authentic liberation is a product of Divine creation, and not merely human ideology. The prophets of ancient Israel linked the doing of justice with divine liberation. For us it means going beyond scholarly debates and presentations about liberation, and becoming "liberative." Since Jesus has taken His place at the very core of history, then the time is long overdue for His followers to take their place beside Him. It means sacrificing our very being in order to be for freedom.

To be for freedom, liberation, indeed, must be a two-edged sword, for oppression has two aspects. The shackles of oppression must be broken (external) while the oppressors are liberated from oppression within (internal). We have been called to seek the "peace" of the city in which we are exiled. For the time being that address is inner city U.S.A. The goal of Divine liberation is the creation of authentic life. There is no authentic life apart from God who has revealed Himself in Jesus Christ "For in Him was life" says the writer of John. As an incomparable Teacher, Jesus does not merely point to authentic life in some specific direction, or to some body of sacred writ reserve for posterity. In comparison to other religious teachers, our blessed Lord is the only Teacher able to say "I am the WAY the TRUTH and the LIFE" (John 14:6). While other teachers attempt to prove their authenticity by appealing to specific proofs, Christ merely says "Verily, verily, I say unto you." There is so much salvific, dynamic energy and life flowing and pulsating through His person, that only He can point to Himself as the source of authentic life.

If we are to transform our cities it must begin with authentic, pulsating, triumphant life. The Kingdom which is none other than the rule of God expressed in history must touch our urban cities. It must touch the political arena, the halls of power, both locally and in the White House and on to the United Nations. It must touch the global village of nations. It must touch every aspect of societal life to the point that "every knee shall bow and tongue confess that Jesus Christ is Lord." In the words of E. Stanley Jones, "the Kingdom of God is realism.....it is coming all the time as people receive it, coming as silent as the dawn. It steals through the thinking and purposes of [men] like leaven, stirring, changing and redeeming. [9]

The urban poor must be empowered to speak on their own behalf. After setting forth the fine task model of the church, namely, call and commitment [*Kerygma*], community and covenant [*Koinonia*], celebration and creativity [*leitourgia*], conscience and challenge [*propheteia*], and care and concern [*diakonia*], using the metaphor of a web suggesting their interconnectedness Robert Pazmino makes a rather telling point. That, "we must choose whether we will accept the responsibility to care for the poor, as we have done in the past. That, the option of caring for the poor does not eliminate the need for ministry at all socioeconomic levels, but it poses a question of how we allocate increasingly limited resources." [10] Writing from an evangelical perspective, as a Christian educator, Pazmino has made an excellent case.

The urban poor must be empowered to speak on their own behalf

In the matter of servanthood, the Kingdom ideal comes to bear. According to our Lord, *"those who will be great among you, let him be your minister,*

And whosoever will be chief among you let him be your servant" [Matt 20:27, 28]. The passion for servanthood cannot be taught. Solidarity with the urban "permanent underclass" a euphemism for the chronic poor, is primary, but such identification is useless unless it can be concretized. God's actions in the city must be concretized in a specific way. We must find a way for faith. Love is a sign, a manifestation of the depth and reality of faith at work. It is the sign of living and acting faith. Faith, without works is dead. Throughout the New Testament, love is given primacy, not faith. [11]

The litmus test for the church will ultimately depend upon the congruence between our word and deed. Servant/deed ministry may take various forms. It means creatively finding a way to empower the underclass. This became most apparent the summer of 1992 just after the Los Angeles riots, while teaching a modular class on Urban Ministry in Van Nuys at Church on the Way where Jack Hayford is Senior Pastor. The question constantly came up. What can we do as a suburban church group to make a difference in the inner city? What we discovered during that intensive class, is that the first thing we must do is to unlearn much of what we have learned either through second-hand information and even through professors who are out of step with the urban ethos. We also learned that in order to arrive at the right solutions, one must raise the right questions.

Those who live on the fringes of the inner-city are challenged to contribute directly or indirectly. On the other side of Cincinnati is the Good News Church of God in Christ where Senior Pastor James Quick shepherds God's people. This church is symbolic of a "stable" ministry that reflects the caring heart of its Pastor. I predict that this church will make its major impact in the near future because the leader is attentive to God. Union Temple Baptist under the leadership of Dr. Willie Wilson in the Anacostia section of the District of Columbia is making its statement in a unique Afro-centric way as it engages political concerns.

While the church is not the Kingdom of God it does act as its agent on earth. Far too many Christians have been so preoccupied with "mansions above" they have forgotten God's interest in creating livable communities here on earth as we operate under the grace and justice of His invisible Kingdom. There is a sense in which we are called and obligated to participate with God in the total cosmic reconciliation of all things including urban America. The church at its best should be a sign of God in the world a sign that God cares about the world. To live under the reign of God is to care in appropriate ways for those who have been brutalized and victimized in life.

A few suggestions are appropriate:

1. Enter the Inner City with a learning attitude

It is the utmost arrogance to enter the inner-city with answers to questions no one is asking. This happens when we enter as an expert and not as a student. Who is better equipped to talk about pain than the urban poor who do not keep a closet full of tranquilizers? Who is better equipped to talk about patience than the urban poor, since "tribulation worketh patience?" Those who serve must be willing to learn from those whose pain they have come to relieve.

2. Make correct social analysis

A prerequisite for strategic ministry in the inner-city is fact finding and information gathering. Marshal accurate data in order to construct a realistic strategic response. When the facts are accurate, the plan of attack can be launched. Find out what is happening in the streets of your neighborhood, city or community. Above all be tutored by the facts.

3. Develop a realistic strategic ministry plan

Develop a plan that is socially realistic, biblically sound and achievable. Short-term and "quick fix" remedies are not effective in the urban setting. In many instances urban problems are deeply pathological and generational. There are families who have been tied to welfare for a long period of time. Their parents were on welfare.

4. Be proactive rather than reactive

When an urban crisis occurs, collective guilt is aroused. A long term assault must be directed toward the structural evil that lies at the base of the urban crises. There is little room for experimentation. We used to say, "an ounce of prevention is worth a pound of cure." Remain proactive as a body.

5. Seek and develop new forms of ministry

During the last three decades, the urban environment has undergone significant change in terms of its politics, composition and lifestyle. In the Los Angeles basin, many African-Americans have moved to newly exploding valley communities, selling their homes and businesses to newly arriving Latinos and Asians. Jesus admonished us that new wine will burst an old wineskin. Today we must reassess the new urban constituencies and develop parallel ministries that address real life-and-death issues. Bread and justice are crucial. One without the other creates a serious void.

For Dialogue and Reflection

1. What ought to be the church's response (especially African-American churches) to African independent churches coming to America?

2. What ought to be the church's response to crime, police insensitivity, mis-education and racism within urbia?

3. In what way (s) can the church participate in confronting racism in our time?

5. Discuss ways in which the church can more effectively participate in the task of humanizing the city?

PART II

CLOSE THE BACKDOOR OF YOUR CHURCH: ON RETENTION

Chapter

6   Revolving Doors: A Challenge for Churches

Recently, many pastors have frankly admitted, *their problem is not with members joining the church.....it's keeping them there."* Most pastors, if honest, will usually admit that this problem has plagued their ministries at one time or another. Whenever *members leaving* equals *members joining*, the church remains the same. Usually the growth and developmental process becomes stunted. I overheard a preacher describe with disgust the two membership drives he has each year. He wistfully intoned, *at the beginning of the year I drive some in, and at the end of the year I drive some out.*

To be honest, the problem of retention is a perennial challenge that cannot be fully resolved one hundred percent....the attrition can be reduced through creative endeavor and prayer

Many church growth theorist tend to agree that assimilation is the key concept that must be thoroughly understood, tenaciously pursued and fully implemented, if new members are to be retained. The term assimilation means *to make like or alike: to incorporate.* The challenge that will not leave begins the day new converts come to Christ. To be honest, the problem of retention is a perennial challenge that cannot be fully resolved one hundred per cent. However, the attrition rate of leaving can be reduced and the problem minimized by approaching it prayerfully and creatively.

Sooner or later, pastors discover that there are some problems and challenges that simply do not evaporate overnight, they just hang around as though they have a peculiar mission to fulfill. After over twenty five years of pastoral ministry in three cities, Philadelphia, Atlanta and Los Angeles, some challenges hang on like an albatross around the neck. There are challenges that stretch our faith, try our commitment and help to make us all that God intended. Most of us have had a plethora of problems that come packaged in many forms. Big ones, small ones, medium size..... challenges prompt us to trust God and draw on our creative imagination that would otherwise lie dormant as we attempt to resolve them.

As a lad in elementary school located in what was then called the "Pompano Projects" nestled in a small town on Florida's East Coast, we were constantly surrounded by migrant workers coming and going from many places. I recall an incident where the school "bully" would constantly intimidate several of us small guys who were pretty mild mannered. We were from a newly developed area called the "Seaboard." For several weeks, as soon as school was out, the "bully" would chase us for dear life. One day our small clan from the "Seaboard" held a small informal conference and decided that if we merely re-doubled our efforts, we perhaps could subdue this guy.

Even though he towered above us in sheer size, our carefully planned strategy involved the element of surprise. As soon as school was out the "bully" came out of no where and made the mistake of chasing us into an open field in the direction of home. At a given signal we turned and headed straight for him. That was half the battle. As the "bully" nearly froze in his tracks, we knew that he had been psychologically disarmed. The rest was up to us as we wrapped and tied him up in knots and proceeded to put one "whipping" on him. That day we emerged as heroes as everyone got a good lick in. We had developed the ability to creatively devise a life-saving strategy during what appeared to have been an eternal life threatening moment. It is no less significant for the church of Jesus Christ as we face the "bully" challenge of church retention. It is a challenge that refuses to leave.

The challenge of retention is tantamount to the problem Israel faced during the period of the Judges as they confronted the Philistines. The Philistines were a warring tribe who lived on the west side of Canaan along the seacoast. From the time of Sampson to the reign of David they were the major enemy force in the land posing a direct threat to the welfare of Israel. They proved to have a distinct advantage over Israel as a warring tribe. They were not only larger in numerical strength, they had mastered the secret technology of making iron weapons. The only real problem they faced was that God was not fighting for them. God raised up Sampson to deal with an enemy who refused to go a way.

In order to effectively attack the problem of church retention, a congregation must redouble its strength and devise various strategies to combat this giant. It is not an impossible task, but it is one that requires commitment, vision, strategy and consistency. It can be done!

Revolving Doors: A Challenge for Churches

Nearly two decades ago, Lyle Schaller, a modern church analyst described the challenge of *retention* by placing it within the context of a discussion about assimilating new members into the church, which was the title of his book. The problem of *retention* was so challenging for Schaller, that he used the metaphor of glue to make his point, by asking rhetorically, *what is the glue that holds congregations together for long periods of time?* According to Schaller:

Once a congregation passes the 50 to 65 level in worship attendance one or both of two patterns begin to emerge. In some congregations the ratio of participation to size begins to decline as the membership figure climbs. The larger that membership total, the lower the ratio of worship attendance to membership. In other congregations this pattern at least partially offset by one or more forces that tend to increase the cohesiveness of the group. When the congregation reaches the 70 to 100 level in worship attendance, it usually is very helpful to examine the sources of this sense of unity. It is even more important to consider this factor when a congregation begins to decline in outreach and size[1]

It is a recognized fact that a great deal of anonymity exists in congregations that begin to exceed three hundred people. That is the reason many people find real security within small to medium churches. Few people enjoy being known as a statistic. Interpersonal relationships continue to carry significant value. People continue to respond to loving, caring relational churches where the pastor can touch his people. Such a church is the Mt Paran Church of God situated in the northern part of Atlanta under the guidance of Dr. Paul Walker, recently elected General Overseer of the Church of God.

Fond in my memories are the moving spirit of this great church during the early seventies during my sojourn in that city. Even today, while huge in size,(estimated 13,000) one can find a sense of warmth, friendliness and community in the spirit of its leader who has had a faithful ministry.

By no means do I mean to suggest that the reverse is always the norm in larger churches. It need not be so if a church is prepared to cope with the *challenge* that will not simply go away. Identifying the source of unity is the key to resolving this perennial *challenge* that will not evaporate. The church must be able to identify the "glue" that holds a congregation together for the long journey of faith. A different kind of "glue" is needed in today's environment.

In today's urban environment, "superglue" is needed if the church is to creatively handle the *challenge of retention*. Human nature has not changed, but the challenges we face are different and often take on myriad appearances. Secularity has impacted our society in such a way that even the church reels from its impact. We must minister to persons whose minds are constantly bombarded by the secular media which is often capitalistic, market driven and for the most part self-serving.

The average commercial on basic television channels does not advertise a simple product unless it is tied to the exploitation of a woman's body in a bikini displaying "skimpy" bare tops. Secular songs bombard the minds of youth with lyrics that would have been too debasing and shameful to utter two decades ago when Schaller described the "glue" needed to hold churches together. Ratings in the media industry are based on the fact that sex sells.

Red Flags, Red Herrings and Back Door Loss

If you converse with the average pastor, regardless to the size of the congregation, they will usually confess that back door loss is a stubborn perennial problem. Many have even admitted that during high moments of successful growth and expansion, new members will leave as soon as they arrive if no meaningful plan is in place to address the problem. Members have even asked where are those new members who joined a few months ago. Officers have complained that they must have exited through the revolving door. Has anyone heard from them?

Revolving door loss has caused some of the most well intentioned church leaders to wring their hands in despair as they attempt to cope with this problem. Caring leaders who are in love with people are usually distraught when revolving door loss occurs. Most responsible pastors will conduct exit interviews for departing members when leaving is eminent. If a member departs without a valid reason, most solid pastors will view this as a negative event. Pastors must exercise discernment, caution and maturity.

What we must realize is that the very best members may very well have valid and legitimate reasons for leaving your church. Compounding back door loss is the fact that this a mobile society. Jobs are down-sized, misfortunes occur, families move with employment opportunities in the public, private and military sector. Families move further away from the urban swirl of life, often characterized by impersonal relationships.

Complicating back door loss are such things as the personality of both pastor and congregation. Some people discover after a brief time in some churches that they simply do not fit. Many church members spend quality time seeking a church that is efficiently organized, people-centered and friendly. There are persons seeking anonymity, so they seek a larger congregation. There are persons who "fit' better in a smaller setting where they can receive personal attention both from pastor and people. It is difficult to love at a distance.

There are times when sudden changes in church programming can often become a point of tension for especially senior members who are deeply emotionally attached to their environment. Members should be prepared for ministry program changes. Once members are given a sense of ownership within an atmosphere of trust they will process rapid changes differently and in a more responsible manner.

When members do not feel emotionally involved in specific tasks where they can make what they deem to be significant contributions to the life and witness of the church tensions and hostilities can develop. Controlling cliques can be a source of discomfort for persons seeking an atmosphere of authentic freedom. It has been well-documented that small power groups within a congregation become dominant in the absence of strong leadership. Strong pastors usually communicate a strong message that they can be compassionately touched, but not manipulated by cliques within the church.

Revolving door loss can be minimized by pastoral leaders who are willing to love, care and share deeply a ministry of special compassion. Pastoral leaders must come to understand that they are stewards entrusted for a brief time with the awesome task of nurturing God's people to maturity. For when revolving door loss equals front door gains, your congregation will remain the same size. Endemic structural problems will not just vanish by mere wishing. Internal conflict, interpersonal tensions, disagreements on priorities, leadership struggle or a combination of other problems beneath the surface may contribute to the stunted growth and loss of parishioners. Certain members may simply "self-destruct" by remaining with your church. Others may move on to greater maturity by leaving.

Pastors should avoid using the pulpit to "whip" members in line

Pastoral leaders should never use the pulpit to "whip" members in line. I have watched churches with large membership take a downward spiral because pastoral leaders did not use wisdom in communicating to their people. Using the pulpit to vent one's personal anger is a sure way to empty a church. We must remember while the people you minister to are children of God, they are not your "children." The pulpit should never be used to demean, humiliate and "beat" upon God's people. The wise counsel of Scripture is to *"be angry but sin not."*

To develop an effective ministry a covenental relationship of caring and mutual respect must exist between pastor and people. Within such a relationship God mediates his grace during stressful times and renders the power necessary for fruitful living. One must possess more than professional training in order to develop a quality relationship with members. It takes time to build a qualitative positive relationship with members. Anyone who attempts a rush job will be in for a great surprise. Most people desire to be respected, valued and loved for who they are. A kind of symbiotic bonding must take place between pastor and people in order to insure a healthy relationship. The authority base of a leader expands when people realize that they are valued in a non-selfish way.

When other concerns come before people disastrous consequences can result. Pastor's are encouraged to assign priority to establishing a relationship of mutual trust and respect for those to whom they minister. Anything other than a healthy relationship raises 'red flags" in the Community of Faith. No ministry can be effective when it is merely a battle ground. When a pastor functions like a one man band "red herrings" will result. It is dangerous for a pastor to make all the decisions.

Using Failure to Your Advantage

Several generations ago the "glue" may have been gummier, but our forbears were able to cope with *challenges* that would not go a way. Richard Allen (1760 - 1831), of the African Methodist Episcopal Church, born into slavery, faced many *challenges* that would not leave. Upon visiting Philadelphia to preach in 1786, decided to leave Delaware, join St. George Episcopal Church and engage in ministry among African-Americans in that city. Allen later wrote, *I soon saw a large field open in seeking and instructing my African brethren who had been a long forgotten people, and few of them attend worship.*

It was Allen who later opposed the virulent poison of racism in the Body of Christ in a protest at the altar of the prominent St. George Church. Allen had the insight to recognize a problem in the Body of Christ, and the foresight to face a problem that would not leave. Today Allen is recognized as a true Black Apostle of freedom for the candor and courage he exemplified in the face of a problem that would not go away.

Charles Grandison Finney (1792 - 1875), faced a major challenge when he left a promising law career in 1821 after receiving *a retainer from the Lord to plead His cause,* and thereby initiated a new era of revivalism. Finney was repeatedly criticized after speaking out against slavery and alcohol. He responded with published arguments and successful evangelistic campaigns. He once wrote, *a revival of religion is not a miracle. It is not a miracle, or dependent on a miracle in any sense... a revival is the result of the right use of the appropriate means.* Finney identified his soul winning strategies as *New Measures,* including praying for sinners by name, holding meetings for unlimited periods of time, permitting women to pray in the meetings and initiating the *anxious bench* for those wanting to repent and receive Christ as Lord. By persisting with stubborn challenges Finney literally led thousands of persons to Jesus Christ.

Dwight Lyman Moody (1837 - 1899), a leading Evangelist of his time, once remarked, *I look upon this world as a wrecked vessel. God has given me a lifeboat and said to me Moody save all you can.* With impetus from God's challenge to him, Moody traveled some one million miles during his entire ministry and established a number of educational institutions, the most renowned one, Chicago Bible Institute, which is today Moody Bible Institute. Through a profound faith in God, Moody learned how to cope with *challenges* that would not go away.

Billy Sunday (1862 - 1935), born in an Iowa log cabin, later gaining notoriety and prominence as a professional baseball player. Between 1912 and 1918, emerged as America's most popular preacher in his vitriolic campaign against a *challenge* that would not go a way, namely alcohol. Sunday once remarked, *I'm trying to make America so dry that a man must be primed before he can spit.* Sunday is perhaps best remembered for attempting to call this nation to moral consciousness during a period of wanton and corrupt living. Even though his prominence receded during the final days of his life, Sunday persisted toward a *challenge* that would not go away. He was committed to the cause of proclamation.

William J. Seymour, best revered as an African-American catalyst for the renowned Los Angeles Azusa Street Revival of 1907, faced a *challenge* that seemingly would not go away; a bolted door, designed to keep him from proclaiming the unsearchable riches of the Kingdom discovered in his new found relationship with the Holy Spirit. After the challenge of the bolted door, Seymour conducted a revival in a converted livery stable that lasted for three years. People from more than fifty nations came, received the baptism in the Holy Spirit, thus catapulting Pentecostals into a global framework. Seymour will be remembered in the annals of history and in the hearts of believers for having used failure to his advantage.

There are people who will wait for perfect conditions before they attempt anything for God. Remember when you wait for perfect conditions, nothing significant ever gets accomplished. Risk taking is inherent in the process of following Jesus Christ. Allen, Moody, Sunday, Graham and Seymour shared a common quality. They had fierce courage in facing formidable challenges. They were not driven by money, buildings, programs, personality and tradition. They valued their calling and viewed their commitment to ministry as primary. Even though failure comes our way, we must take the high road achieving our goals because God is faithful.

Billy Graham faced an ominous challenge as youthful Evangelist in a revival meeting held in Los Angeles in 1949. After three weeks of rainy weather, the meeting was virtually declared a failure. William Randolph Hearst called his Chief Editor of the Los Angeles Times and merely instructed them to "puff Graham." [2] Those two words launched Graham into national spotlight. After launching the famous Hour of Decision radio broadcast in 1950, Graham has preached to more than 100 million people in more than 100 countries around the world. From the challenge of a failed revival during a rain soaked week, Graham has played a key role in shaping the ethos of evangelism in modern times. Through a discipline heart, mind and spirit combined with a love for the Lord, Graham learned how to *use failure to his advantage* in ministry.

Every church must decide whether it will flounder, fizzle or flourish

Failure has been defined so many ways and means different things to different people. Failure can be an unsuccessful attempt at performing a particular task. To fail in a certain context is to abort, collapse, default, decline, desert, disappoint, flounder, quit, wither, miscarry, and to breakdown. Every church must decide whether it will flourish or fizzle. It cannot do both effectively. Just as every pastor must decide whether she/he will run or reign. You cannot do both. Ilka Chase once said, *the only people who never fail are those who never try.* We might benefit from the wisdom of the great American inventor, Thomas Edison who once said, *show me a thoroughly satisfied man and I will show you a failure.*

The greatest lessons of my life were learned from situations where I simply had failed. Contrary to popular wisdom that says, "winners never quit." There are times when winners quit, but it is only temporary. a winner will analyze failure and think through the meaning and implication of each aspect of the challenge. John Salak was correct, *failures are divided into two classes....those who thought and never did, and those who did and never thought.* The key to retention is freedom. People must be given the freedom to exit. The human spirit tends to resent an imprisoning environment. The mind can become awfully creative when it intuits that one's freedom is endangered. Have you ever watched an animal entrapped against its will? God forbid that it turns out to be a porcupine or a skunk. Someone remarked that a bull dog can whip a skunk but its just not worth the effort. You will pay a price for entrapment! Members must be respected and given the freedom to leave your ministry.

Members Must Be Free To Leave

Usually when members are given the freedom to leave, they will remain and attempt to work out the difficulty. Antoine De Saint-Exupery once said, *I know but one freedom and that is the freedom of mind.* Freedom is one of the values we cherish most in our time because it is often the gateway to other benefits of human existence. To be free is to be unobstructed, unchained, unfettered, liberated and released. Since authentic freedom does not come easy, there is a sense of security that becomes the payoff for embracing it. Religious liberty is a value we cherish dearly because religion is bound up with the emotions. The same holds true for congregations, regardless to size.

I recently listen to a prominent pastor during a Sunday morning worship service challenge those members who were complaining about the city and were contemplating leaving......to leave. At first, as I listened I thought that this appeared on the surface to be cold, callous, cruel and heartless. But after thinking it through, I was able to clearly discern what this pastor was doing. He was merely giving members the freedom to do what they had clearly telegraphed from time to time. Let's suppose for a moment that this same pastor would have started a pity party for himself combined with an attempt to fence in all those who were planning their departure. Such futile attempts can only result in cruel and unusual treatment for members of the Community of Faith.

Even God does not violate the integrity of our will. It is another way of saying that God will not force us to serve Him against our will. Perhaps the Apostle Paul had the freedom that God gives when he wrote: *So Christ has made us free. Now make sure that you stay free and don't get all tied up again in the chains of slavery to Jewish laws and ceremonies.* (LAB

Galatians 5:1) Freedom is not licentiousness, for that would be a new form of enslavement. We are now free to do what was impossible before. We have a new Master who has given us freedom.

One of the worst things a pastor can do when members decide that they are leaving is to set what I call an entrapment mode. Over a period of years I have watched pastors who have received hints of members about to leave do everything from pleading to literally entrapping them. Some pastors literally block members with enticing positions in leadership roles created on the spot that only turn out to be perfect sources for continued problems. Others begin the process of giving members who hint of leaving extra attention. This is a time of crisis for both pastor and people.

Unfortunately, with all the niceties afforded by an already weary and embattled condescending leader, members will invariably leave. We must be courageous enough to explore the reasons why members move on to other ministries. The *first* thing a pastor should do is get calm. Do not panic! You will learn a few things about human nature that you will not find in seminary text books. Once you prayerfully ascertain the reason particular members are leaving, keep accurate records for future reference. The *second* thing of importance, is to avoid debate and confrontation about the stated reasons presented. Remember, the stated reasons are not always the real reasons.

Sometimes there are hidden agendas that will eventually emerge if you are patient and willing to be a good pastoral listener to what is also unstated. *Thirdly,* compassionately release departing members to go. As you imbue them with the gift of freedom, pray for God's grace to be with them. *Fourthly,* try as the situation will permit to resolve personal issues so that members can truly depart free, in order to become spiritually productive in future ministry. Failure to resolve personal issues can result in years of pronounced tension and hostility. I have observed parishioners who for reasons of unresolved issues go on for years without reciprocating with other Christians. Such tensions are like hardening arteries, apart from serious medical therapy, the condition becomes progressively worse.

Members should be given the freedom to depart from a ministry in peace

Your long range goal is to have a matured spiritual relationship with members who have departed your ministry without displaying malice, spite or jealousy. Ultimately, members must be free to pursue different paths without any interference. You cannot be free until they have been set free. Likewise, they cannot be free until you have become free. Please do not procrastinate with seething hostilities between members who have made their decisions and are looking forward to being released. God is not the Author of confusion, so states the Holy Writ. God is a God of peace. As believers we are simply called to believe, but also to belong.

That really means that we belong to each other even though we may have to go separate ways. *Pastors....learn from the experience!* Once members learn that there is no such thing as a church free from problems they will make matured decisions. There will always be something to contend with in every congregational setting. A good pastoral leader can minimize problem areas within the church by wisdom, skill and excellent planning. The **Zion Baptist Church**, distinguished as the oldest African Baptist church founded by slaves in Marietta, Georgia under the leadership of Dr. Harris Travis is a good example of a church honestly seeking to deal with interpersonal problems and succeeding.

For Dialogue and Reflection

1. Is there a "revolving- door" syndrome in your church?

2. Are leaders perceived as "bosses" in your church?

3. Discuss the downside of using the pulpit to "bully" or demean people?

4. Is there risk-taking when members are given the freedom to leave?

CHAPTER
7 BOLTING ALL SIDE DOORS

Handling Small Things that Matter
When members decide to leave for whatever reasons they will depart through any door that is open. There are certain side door concerns that need to be examined. To be comprehensive, we must also be aware of this reality. Once dissatisfied members enter the fault finding mode, there is a point where nothing really satisfies or is really right, and it may very well not be the leaders fault. However we should do all that we can to launch a good offensive. One way is to do preventive kinds of things that entail side door issues. There are many more to add to our list and you should sit and think creatively about what may be a side door concern in your ministry.

► *Let's Park our Automobile*
Parking is important! Whether you are planning to purchase or build, make sure that you give parking priority in your future plans. It is a given, people tend not to worship where parking is a real problem. It can make or break a potentially great ministry. Building codes in most cities usually have strict requirements for new buildings with regards to adequate parking. In a consumer-oriented society convenience is important. Robert Schuller of the Crystal Cathedral in Garden Grove California from the inception of his ministry, assigned priority to parking, and ....did it pay off?

Churches have invested in parking lot attendants to make sure automobiles are parked safely and secure. It is not uncommon to see attendants using walkie talkies to communicate as they give attention to parking details at a church in Fort Lauderdale, Florida. This church has been cited for the attention it gives to persons arriving for worship. Friendly attendants even open the doors for visitors and escort you to the front door, where ushers take charge and further escort you to your choice seat. Assign significant value to parking and watch the positive shift in church attendance.

One experiences a deep sense of satisfaction in knowing that your automobile is secure and safe as worship takes place. On the other hand one can experience deep anxiety knowing that one's automobile is not safe and that any personal belonging may also be lost. While insurance may prove important, it is the threat of loss that raises the anxiety level of most well meaning persons. It is most unfortunate in our time that thieves also target churches as a place to commit petty crimes. Many churches are fighting back with vigilant brave youth who are not afraid of confrontation after having been on the streets for years. When potential thieves realize that they are in for major confrontation as they approach unsuspecting church people, they will more than likely change their *modus operandi*. In cities such as Philadelphia, Washington D.C., Los Angeles, it is not uncommon to hear church people espousing such phrases as "taking back" the territory that Satan has taken. Believe me, they are taking that phrase seriously as evil is confronted even in such matters as making a parking lot safe for those who dare to worship God.

Some churches have developed adequate parking to accommodate their increasing numbers. Some cities have very strict building regulations and codes that take into consideration such issues as parking for the future. Parking spaces are geared toward the seating capacity of your church. I recall having to go through the bureaucratic red tape of a local township in order to secure a variance in order to proceed with a specific project. We were able to secure a variance after several hearings and the cooperation of neighbors. For a church to provide adequate parking is not an expense but rather a long term investment.

My personal experience when arriving at a church where I am to minister may not be normative. However I recall the many times I have registered personal concern over the safety of my automobile. My concern had much more to do with preventing an inconvenience than materialism. We do not like to be inconvenienced. People are no longer safe at shopping malls where

Bolting All Side Doors 93

security is "beefed up" during holiday seasons. Yet auto losses take place significantly even in the presence of security. I read where a certain mall in suburban Philadelphia had three hundred plus autos stolen during 1995. At church we have a feeling of well being when we know that the parking area is well lighted and relatively safe.

A dark or poorly lighted parking lot is an open invitation to hoodlums to burglarize automobiles. During my first year as pastor in Los Angeles, I recalled staying later than usual one evening to take care of a few tasks that I had omitted earlier in the day. At dusk I heard the sound of a hood latch springing open. I cautiously approached the car from the rear. I saw the form of an individual who had also seen me. It was a surprised potential thief. He took off running up the alley with all deliberate speed. We increased lighting on the lot and placed a timer on the switch. Members no longer felt unsafe and attendance increased.

▸ *Why Security is Important*

The steadily increasing crime rate has raised additional concerns about the importance of security for persons attending church. a few decades ago, such a concern was rarely mentioned. In today's contemporary urban environment, security must be assigned significant value. If people do not feel safe they will not attend. I first encountered this as a concern while pastoring in Los Angeles. Thieves are extremely bold today and often function in a reckless manner without regard for human life. We have encountered thieves attempting to burglarize automobiles during worship services. A friend reported that thieves entered his brother lot and stole pit bulls that were guarding the facility. Thieves do not respect alarms and clubs on automobiles. Somehow they find a way to disengage most security mechanisms.

Many churches cannot afford to hire full time security services to cover worship times. We resolved our security problem by pooling our manpower on a voluntary basis. We had men rotating constantly to provide a monitoring circle of surveillance. When potential thieves discovered that we were also watching, they retreated. Today, you may invest in a surveillance camera for your parking lot and utilize one or more persons to monitor and report any suspicious activity. Some churches utilize the "buddy system" where people who are in attendance at special functions travel in groups. Other churches utilize the "escort system" as a sure means of security from building to automobile.

While it is a sad commentary on the state of society, we must be positive as we confront the kingdom of evil in every way in our fallen world. Prayer must be combined with security. As Christians we continue to believe that guardian angelic beings "encamp" around those who fear God. We must pray diligently for the city. Except the Lord keep the city "the watchman waketh but in vain."

As I skimmed the Metro section of the daily news tabloid, I noticed an article describing two Maryland teenagers who had been arrested in Virginia for a gunpoint car jacking at a famous suburban shopping Mall. They were apprehended at a well known fashion center at Pentagon City as they tried to use a stolen credit card. This Mall attracts approximately 60,000 shoppers on an average December day. According to law enforcement specialists, such Malls are beginning to experience more serious crime. The incident involvement two young men, one brandishing a pistol approaching a man sitting in his car. In the end two 16 year olds were charged with credit card fraud and robbery car-jacking. They had been charged as juveniles and police did not release their names. [1]

What is so incredible is that a large number of serious crime are committed by teenagers. What a challenge for the church! Many of these young people have already been incarcerated often with a lengthy rap sheet. As we think about security concerns may we also focus on the church's challenge to save our youth. Last year I had the privileged of leading a young teenager to Christ known only as "Broadway." At the altar I went eyeball to eyeball with Broadway telling his "this is your day." I was not intimidated by his dred lock hair style and baggy pants. I had that gut feeling that here was a leader. I struck gold on that Sunday morning. Not only did God save "Broadway' but four of his old buddies made commitments to follow Jesus Christ. I saw "Broadway" several months later and did not recognize him except that I remembered his eyes. Pastor Sutton and his wife Bertha (an elementary school principal) of the Maryland Church of God in Christ have developed a serious mentoring relationship with former street guys. The criminal justice system has failed in many ways because it is only a partial solution to criminality. We can purport values that can make the difference for youth who have not been impacted by the criminal justice system.

▸ *How Does Your Community View Your Church?*

In most instances it does matter what people think about the place we worship if we are honest. We must ask, how is our church perceived in our

Bolting All Side Doors 95

immediate community? Is our worship facility perceived as an eyesore on the block or a compliment to the community. Church leaders should seek to improve the physical appearance of their place of worship with as much enthusiasm as possible. In the Old Testament, Solomon invested a great deal of physical resources in building a Temple unto the Lord. Eliminating a "we don't care look" from your worship facility can mean your survival in the long run. Building cosmetics can transform an eyesore into a place of beauty and dignity with wise planning even with limited financial resources.

Every church by its physical appearance makes a statement. Such a statement is viewed either negative or positive by the readers of the immediate community. It is ironic that many Christian leaders spend megabucks on their homes while the House of God falls apart for lack of tender loving care. As a child I recall persons devoting many hours of free time to cleaning the sanctuary and making sure that it would make the right statement by sheer appearance alone. In those days members did not expect pay for every task performed. We have a generation of persons who refuse to perform simple task without expecting financial remuneration for services performed. Volunteerism should always be a live option for today's Christian. The place we choose to worship ought to reflect the dignity of holiness. When a community develops a negative perception of the church it is unusually difficult to counter.

► *Does Information Flow Through Your Church?*

How is the information flow in your church? In this time of information glut and a focus on information super highways, computers, ROM's (read-on-memory), and other information technology, there is no reason for an ill informed constituency. Are members correctly informed in your church? Is your community appropriately informed? When members are adequately informed they will respond positively. It is important to make sure your immediate community is adequately informed about your presence, mission and ministry.

Have you ever designed a brochure for your ministry? Was it realistically descriptive? Was it given to first time visitors and mailed to prospects? Today, you can call an 800 number and in one day you can have information sent to your address that can assist you in delivering a brochure more than adequate for your need. Several months after I was installed at Crossroads Church in Los Angeles, we were able to formulate a brochure that described our vision of ministry for the first three years. It becomes a kind of informal paper contract. Members can use brochures to nudge the leadership about their progress and movement toward announced goals. Brochures are excellent vehicles for improving information flow to your congregation and your immediate community.

The key point to remember in developing an information brochure, is to describe what you are doing in a realistic way so that it will generate enthusiasm among your constituency. I have read brochures passed out by churches that were not reality based. It is important that the truth about what you are envisioning get to the right sources, but more importantly that you remain credible as a representative for our Lord and His Kingdom. Keep information flowing and watch the enthusiasm increase about your ministry objectives.

Ours is an information age. The ever present Internet is with us. Information is now at our finger tips. Information glut is not uncommon. You do not need a web page on the Internet in order to keep information flowing through your church. In most congregations, one can usually find a computer 'buff' who enjoys handling information. Why not try creating a position for a church information specialist. Such persons can accomplish enormous tasks when given minimal support. Information can be passed on through a well developed news letter. With the use of desk top publishing utilizing graphics one can create an attractive information brochure.

Chapter

8 FROM THE INSIDE OUT:
Evaluating Five Key Areas of Ministry

Urban Ministry Outreach : Reaching the Underside at Whatever Cost

Evangelism has to do with the means we employ to lead persons to a saving knowledge of Jesus Christ as Lord and to effect wholeness in one's total humanity. It is with conviction that I urge churches to link Evangelism with Urban Ministry in order to provide a full orb ministry. As you inventory this aspect of your ministry, begin by honestly assessing the current status of Evangelism in your church. For many churches there is no organized effort of concerted witness to the world. Evangelism is the life blood of the church. In other churches it is left up to each person to chart their own course of action when it comes to Evangelism.

▶ *Does Evangelism have an urban emphasis?*

Pastor Joseph Webb of the Free at Last COGIC in St. Paul, Minnesota has the street smarts wisdom and finesse to win a diverse cadre of individuals to Christ. After a prominent gang member came to Christ in his immediate neighborhood, his church exploded with new growth. Six months after a church development seminar, the church filled to capacity. They recently moved to a new edifice. I predict great things for his fellowship in the immediate future.

The gift of salvation entails wholeness, and wholeness implies that we deal with the totality of one's situation and circumstance in order to effectively sustain persons in today's urban environment. Since the world has come to the city, according to contemporary missiologist, are you geared to reach diverse people groups that have come to our land? The illegal alien has a soul and a destiny also. They must also eat and survive off the land as they come to Jesus Christ. Evangelism must also concern itself with bread and butter concerns if it is to achieve wholeness. Evangelism must also be concerned with the economic deprivation that has invaded so many urban communities if it is to effect wholeness.

> *Are church auxiliaries within your church involved with Evangelism?*

This is a crucial question that really questions your ecclesiology (doctrine of the church) Because Evangelism Outreach is God's grand design, it appears that the church would be remiss not to become involved in its totality. I once decided to critically evaluate the role of every auxiliary in our church, to determine its real function. The rationale was that if it did not have a meaningful value or function it would be considered excess baggage. Needless to say we carefully went through the process of elimination to the utter pain of many only to discover that this process was necessary for the health of the body.

> *Is your Evangelistic approach culturally sensitive?*

Too often we assume that everyone is "just like we are" only to be awakened by sheer reality less we offend others by saying or doing the wrong thing to offend persons who are uniquely different. When reality comes home that everyone is not like we are, the fences go up, the chasm widens and the bridges cave in. Have you honestly thought about the make up of the church of the twenty-first century? Diversity is a reality that we must prepare for on the eve of the turn of the century. Evangelism must seek to build mutual understanding rather than focus solely on where another person "is coming from." Evangelism must bridge differences rather than insist on similarity of perspectives or views. Culture has to do with the sum total of who we really are as social beings.

To become culturally sensitive may mean breaking out of our enslaving cultural ghetto and initiating fellowship with persons who are different. I have discovered over a period of time that the more points of contact that you have in your immediate community, the more people you come in contact with. Sometimes you grow just by simply touching other people in various community organizations. We are enriched by the presence of persons who are different if we process the experience in a positive manner.

> *Is Your Church Engaged in any aspect of World Evangelism?*

There are a variety of ways to connect with World Evangelism. Have you ever tried a concerted response to an effort to bring wholeness to Haiti, the Sudan and Eastern Europe? Most of us have been moved to tears as we watch programs by World Vision and other organizations attempting to bring wholeness to deprived persons. Many of us are prone to turn the TV off as the camera focuses on emaciated children lying death prone on the bare ground in parts of Africa, or abandoned children walking the streets of Brazil and living in sewers. Many of us have watched with a feeling of helplessness, people in Haiti bathing in water infected by human waste and all kinds of bacteria. You will be surprised how your own ministry will reap the fruits of feeding the hungry, for you will indeed be feeding the One who is the Bread of Life.

> *Are you working from the Inside Out?*

A church that works from the "inside out" will not experience the loss and attrition rate of a church that attempts to move people from the "outside in" without giving serious attention to several internal areas. In order to get your church to the level of mission, mandate and maturity, it will be necessary to submit to an evaluation. In medicine it is called a physical, a checkup, involving diagnosis. No sane physician will begin treatment without adequate medical diagnosis. It involves listening, observation, touching and even "poking." Malpractice insurance is expensive to maintain, but is mandatory in the event a physician gives you an aspirin for a stroke, and you live to find out about it.

By now you recognize that this is an evaluation section, designed specifically with your church in mind. There are four more key areas of ministry that should be subjected to inventory if you are to develop the kind of church that attracts and keeps members. They are **Worship** and **Music**, **Christian Nurture** and **Counseling**, **Youth Ministry** and **Stewardship**. In order to effectively *close the back door of your church,* several candid questions must be raised and hopefully, honest answers given. A good physician will ask you to describe your pain as one searches for the proper remedy. It is significant that you render *your version* of your pain. Even though the physician has the diagnostic tools in hand, the questions you answer from *your* perspective are critical for medical therapy and effecting a cure.

- ### *Worship and Music Ministry Inventory: Let's Dance*

Elsewhere I have tried to argue a case for the primacy of worship. [1] Whether or not your worship is Protestant, Pentecostal, Charismatic, Catholic, liturgical, contemporary or traditional, it is foundational and central to all that we do. For in worship we come to grips with our finitude and humanity by recognizing with the Psalmist that, *it is He that hath made us and not we ourselves.* In worship we listen to the still small voice that constantly reminds us that *God is a Spirit and they that worship Him must worship Him in spirit and in truth.*

Metaphorically, worship is like the ocean that feeds the smaller rivers, rivulets, streams and brooks. That is why it is crucial that we have the discernment to know when the *brook of worship* has dried up. That is why authentic worship cannot be restricted to places, times and certain peoples. When authentic worship takes place, you can be assured beyond a reasonable doubt that God will "show up" whether it occurs in a cotton field or cathedral, an altar or auditorium, a storefront or stable, a swamp or seminar. Worship ought never be treated as ancillary or assigned a secondary role in one's plan of ritual and praise to God. Robert Webber has so passionately and eloquently argued for the relevance and place of worship in the schema of adoration to God.

In **_Worship Is a Verb_**, Webber asserts that, *evangelism and other functions of ministry flow from the worship of the church.* [2] It is idolatry when worship is transformed into a "self-aggrandizing" event for "bless me club members" only. God insists upon centrality in the act of worship. During the worship event we enter concert with the Psalmist, *Unto Thee O Lord do we lift up our praise.*

- ### *Is your worship primary?*

Try to answer this question with all the candor and sincerity that you can muster as you seek to *close the back door of your church.* If your answer is no to this question, do not panic. Most churches are in serious trouble on this question for several reasons. a theology of worship usually dictates the place of worship in our hierarchy of spiritual values. The primary task of theology is to clarify the nature of the Christian faith for the believing community.

Since theology is neither right or wrong, but rather *good* or *bad*, we need to critically examine what we believe and think about our attitude toward the God we worship. Is worship in your church assigned a primary role? Will members and visitors leave knowing that they have been confronted by the living God? Does your worship leaders have an essential and comprehensive understanding of the centrality and symbolic meaning of the total worship experience?

▸   *Is your worship inspiring?*

Our goal is to attempt to raise the right questions, rather than provide the right answer. When worship becomes a task or a chore, something is wrong. Do people leave the way they came? Does your worship challenge both members and visitors to get involved without feeling "set upon"? Are people forced to stand in group participation and asked to repeat cliches they may not believe? Are worship participants weary and tired rather than inspired? a worship experience should not sap energy from the participants. From a pastoral perspective, worship should energize participants to go back into the world with the strength and courage to face seemingly impossible and insurmountable tasks. Authentic worship must be the source of all that it takes to make life bearable in a society that is increasingly becoming anti-God. Few moments are as important as a liberating worship experience.

▸   *Is your worship creative?*

Few problems we encounter in church life are really unique to us. Our primary task is not to re-invent the wheel, but rather to share solutions to common problems that have been tried and proven. Are people bored stiff because your worship format has become predictable? Do you use creativity in the selection of songs for worship? Do you ride the same worship "hobby horse" from week to week? We are challenged by the Psalmist to *worship the Lord with a new song.* What a challenge for a dead, hum drum spiritually moribund worship service. Dean Merrill and Marshall Shelley edited a small book under the auspices of Christianity Today, entitled *[Fresh Ideas for Preaching, Worship and Evangelism*, Word Books: Waco, 1984], that can serve as an excellent resource for "beefing" up a worship service that has fallen into a trap.

A fundamental problem I have observed in worship services is that we do not prepare people for the worship event. Creativity should be encouraged in worship. Bishop Flynn Johnson of the expanding Atlanta Metropolitan Church not only leads an awesome worship, but occasionally utilizes his drama team to do the weekly announcements. This pastor has also invested a great deal of time in building internal strength within the congregation by utilizing the cell group concept. I had the opportunity to visit one of these sessions around five o'clock in the evening only to discover that the head of the residence was one of my former Morehouse classmates, Robert Holliman. The meeting was awesome as each person supported each other in a powerful genuine way.

Too often we become so time conscious that the primary meaning for the gathered event slips past us. In 1993 and 1994 I had the rare privilege of participating in several worship services in Accra, Ghana in special conferences convened by the venerable Pastor, catalyst and spiritual leader, Dr. Mensa Otabil. It was the most awe inspiring worship I have witnessed in my life. It was easy to flow with the spiritual current and divine energy released into the atmosphere. The music was balanced, the songs were inspiring, the spontaneity was contagious, and the worshipers were caught up in *kairos* (time charged and pregnant with meaning), rather than *chronos* (clock time). The Holy Spirit was regnant and the worship moment literally caught fire. I could hardly wait to return for the next worship.

▸ *Does Your Church Maintain a Balance between Contemporary and Traditional Modes of Worship?*

To what extent are you attempting to achieve balance between traditional and contemporary forms of worship. The task requires a delicate balancing of the two. It is not unusual to find older matured members embracing more traditional forms of worship. A special workshop on worship would be of tremendous value to worship leaders so as to increase their options. Pastor Stenneth Powell, Senior Minister of the Abundant Life Christian Center, Raleigh, North Carolina, is an excellent resource person for developing a praise and worship format. The praise and worship service at Abundant Life Church is simply awesome!.

▸ *Does Your Evening Worship Service Provide Variety?*

The phrase *"variety is the spice of life'* is more than an old adage, it is reality! An evening service that has variety will lure worshipers back. There are many churches in the urban environment who refuse to have evening worship for a variety of reasons. There is a sense in which your church can capitalize on this. After basic devotionals, try having forums and panels generating appropriate discussions germane and relevant to the needs of those persons in attendance. Have you ever tried having a fireside chat with your congregation without a crisis brewing? Have you ever tried to plan a meaningful communion worship service on a Sunday evening? Try being creative with your use of symbolism for this event.

In Los Angeles at my last pastorate, on first Sunday evenings, we always left communion with a sense of Divine presence and empowerment permeating the atmosphere imbuing us with power for the week. Recently I was moved by the inspiring Sunday evening worship at the Upper Room Church of God In Christ, Raleigh, North Carolina, where Patrick Wooden is the Senior Pastor. It was characterized by spontaneity and variety.

▸ **Does Your Worship Service make Sense to Unbelievers?**

There are times when churches become so self-serving and into their own agenda that they forget their primary mission to the lost and alienated. Unbelievers often come with a value system that is often foreign to the Community of Faith. When unsaved persons strain for meaning, there is a need to make specific adjustments to correct this problem. People tend to be more responsive when they understand the worship format. Do not be afraid to be creative in planning worship services that appeal to unbelievers. The "field is the world" according to our blessed Lord. At the Ebenezer African Methodist Episcopal , Fort Washington, Maryland where Granger and Joy Browning are senior pastors, worship is truly a serious and eventful happening where one experiences authentic liberation.

Music Ministry

▸ **Is Music Perceived as Ministry by Musicians and Choir Members?**

Music Ministry is not a time in the worship service for display, ostentatiousness and show time. Music in worship must be perceived as ministry and not a time for "spiritual exhibitionism." Even in the Old Testament musicians performed a special ministry unto the Lord in Temple worship. Consciousness of one's role in ministry is crucial for the way a specific ministry is rendered. It is as crucial as self-concept for building esteem. Music Ministry must never be reduced to mechanical performance. Music should be viewed as one of the most significant arenas for service in the life of the church. The Music Ministry of a church is the dynamo that radiates levels of energy through the total worshiping community.

Recently I was privileged to serve a seminar week end at the **Cathedral of Fresh Fire**, Wilmington, Delaware under the dynamic leadership of Pastor Emma Creamer. This congregation has been trained to sing difficult praise songs in an inspirational way as capable musicians such as Dr. Ramona Howard and talented gospel singer Tammy Lindsay embellish such singing with awe-inspiring musical background. When Music Ministry is perceived as ministry, the results can be surprising.

▶ **Is Your Minister of Music Resourceful?**

It is mandatory that the person providing leadership for your Ministry of Music be resourceful in every way. Does your Minister of Music do just enough to get by? A competent Minister of Music will perform research, study, visit other ministries, exchange information and attend workshops in order to provide a special quality of Music Ministry to your church. Resourcefulness is a crucial characteristic for the person responsible for the total Music Ministry of the church. During my last pastorate at Crossroads Church in Los Angeles, my Choir Director was always in communication with Travis Aniton, Minister of Music in preparation for the forthcoming worship. I can still see Tyrone Wade, Music Director during difficult times sharing, planning, communicating and preparing for the worship with a deep sense of seriousness as though all depended on him. By keeping the two positions (Director and Minister of Music) separate, we were able to accomplish a great deal more and distribute responsibility evenly. Churches who invest in a resourceful Minister of Music is well on the way toward closing the back door of one's church.

Christian Nurture and Counseling Inventory: Does Anyone Care?

Christian Education (nurture) encompasses the total teaching ministries of the church that enables persons to mature in Jesus Christ. The counselor is also an educator who often teaches by example, by instruction, and by guiding the counselee as he or she learns to cope with life situations. Counseling is not a step-by-step process such as designing a dress, preparing a meal or repairing an automobile. Each counselee is unique with their own particular problems, attitudes, values experiences, hopes, dreams and aspirations that are unlike any other. Churches who invest in Christian Nurture and Counseling are well on their way to closing the back door of their church.

> **Is your ministry of Christian nurture geared toward meeting the needs of your total Faith Community?**

A key in closing the back door of your church is your ability to know the needs of those to whom you minister. In today's religious environment this perennial challenge is forever at the church's door. It means taking the initiative to peer and probe into the lives of parishioners without being a nuisance. It means taking the initiative to highlight the forces that impact your people and constantly utilize the gift of discernment as you lead God's people. Are 'need-driven' ministry of nurture has built in rewards for those who can invest the time and energy in getting to know your people beyond the visceral level on a Sunday.

Many of the people we lead often suffer from psychological, social and geographical dislocation in a mobile society. A ministry of nurture must provide the necessary direction to people who are victimized by an insecure environment. Increasingly the areas to which we are called as Christians no longer are clearly delineated. We must often function in morally shaded grey areas of ambiguity where clear insight is needed. It is precisely in such a world that we must struggle, for it is here that the word of judgment and grace must be spoken. Programmatic response in a relevant way to people concerns in one of the ways to close the back door . Once parishioners decide that a leader cares, there are no restrictions that can be imposed upon the outpouring of love for that leader.

> **Is your ministry of nurture 'culturally sensitive'?**

Ours is an era of a new pluralism on the landscape of North American society with far-reaching consequences. The celebration of one's ethnicity is no longer one of embarrassment, but rather a source of pride. Handling demographic diversity is the new challenge facing North American society. Bilingual educational challenges impact and affect school districts throughout our land, thus raising the prospect of difficult new policy decisions that will impact future generations. Churches are being affected by this new pluralism in various ways. A respectable biblical case can be made for churches that can celebrate their pluralistic character and uniqueness without "constructing a Tabernacle" in its favor. The new climate of diversity favors the development of a ministry of Christian nurture that is culturally sensitive without being obvious.

No longer can ministries of nurture be constructed as though culture were a singular entity. This theological nearsightedness has been the pitfall of the church in recent times. To be effective, relevant and related, Christian nurture must be grounded in a supra cultural gospel that must be incarnated anew each time it addresses diverse people groups.

▸ *Are parishioners opposed to updating traditional methods?*

There are many persons within the borders of the Faith Community who embrace the past in an idolatrous way. Perhaps the temptation is greater when "there are more years behind us than in front of us". When members are categorically opposed to revising traditional methods of nurture, a real problem exists that can have far-reaching implications. If a method or technique is working, continue utilizing it. However if it has no meaning for the present, discard it in the name of sanity.

On the other hand there is nothing that guarantees that a certain method or technique has merit because it is new, it has to be tested against reality. We must continue to subject traditional methods of nurture to the highest form of scrutiny. The critical question must always be the question of meaning in our time. Either meaning is crucial or it isn't. Over two decades ago Dean M. Kelley remarked, *"if meaning is to be central and ultimate, it will take precedence over all other things, including persons. If it does not take precedence over other things, including persons, it will no longer be central and ultimate".[3]* Try to be open to revising traditional methods that demonstrate promise for the future.

▸ *Is Christian Counseling an option in your church?*

Counseling has been viewed as a fulfilling and hazardous occupation. While all believers should demonstrate compassionate concern for humankind, it does not logically follow that all Christians are or can become Christian counselors. Is Christian counseling optional in your ministry? Are you equipped to assist newly converted substance abusers in transitioning to your congregation? What about the proliferation of single parents and their need to center down within an atmosphere of acceptance without fear of being highlighted as obvious?

In today's religious environment, effective Christian counseling is not an option, it is a crucial necessity. The proliferation of serious problems we face today are unlike those of any previous generation. When people are bruised and beaten down by life's circumstances and uncertainties they need specialized help. Friends don't always make the best counselors even though they may be full of advice. An effective Christian counselor enables persons to draw upon their faith and inner resources in order to cope with their pain and work through their crisis. Effective Christian counseling is crucial in closing the back door of your church.

▸ **What characteristics should you look for in a Christian Counselor?**

While there are many well-meaning Christians who have the assurance of eternal life with our Lord, they are not experiencing a full life in this world. For such persons traditional Christian nurturing methods alone are not sufficient to sustain them. According to Gary Collins:

"counseling might help counselees recognize unconscious harmful attitudes, teach interpersonal skills and new behaviors, or show how to mobilize one's inner resources to face a crisis. ......At times such counseling, guided by the Holy Spirit, can free a counselee from hang-ups which prevent one from growing to Christian maturity."[4]

This reinforces the need for the church to recognize its presence as a "healing community' in the midst of a chaotic world. Indeed this is mission and ministry.   Elsewhere, Collins relates a four year study conducted with hospital patients and a variety of counselors it was confirmed that patients improved when their therapists showed high levels of warmth, genuineness and accurate empathic understanding. When counselor qualities were lacking, the hospital patients grew worse.[5]

So crucial are counselor characteristics that Collins lists them in detail. They are *warmth, genuineness* and *empathy*. **Warmth**= *this word implies caring, respecting, or possessing a sincere, non smothering concern for the counselee--regardless of one's attitudes or actions.* **Genuineness**= *genuiness implies spontaneity without impulsiveness and honesty without cruel confrontation. The genuine counselor is "for real"...an open, sincere person who avoids phoniness or the playing of some superior role.* **Empathy**= *This ability to "feel with' the counselee is what we mean by accurate empathic understanding.*[6] A church would do well to invest some quality time in locating an effective Christian Counselor as an important step in closing the back door of your church.

In ministries where firm effective counseling is taking place on a consistent basis it minimizes the interpersonal problems that often causes churches to bog down. Given the nature of the cultural crisis we are experiencing in our time, all of us are impacted in some way. New challenges tend to go underground should we ignore them. Guilt is nothing more than the past made present in our consciousness. Experienced therapist are trained to assist troubled persons in coping with their personal problems.

Pastors are urged to spend time locating competent Christian counselors. One call to a Theological Seminary in your area may be the most important call of your ministry. Competent Christian counseling will underwrite itself in the long run, and God will be glorified. I know several young people who have been trained to engage in Christian counseling and would like the opportunity to make a significant contribution to the work of the church and Kingdom.

Youth Inventory: What's Up DOC?

The primary task of youth ministry is to provide systematic nurture to youth thereby enabling them to fulfill, maximize and realize their full potential through Jesus Christ or Lord.

> **Are we realistically in touch with the world of today's Youth?**

The worst mistake that youth leaders can make today is to generalize about youth with the "youth-will-be-youth" approach. We cannot always assume that youth who are actively involved with church activities are fundamentally different from non-church youth. Merton Strommen, a research psychologist from Minneapolis conducted an extensive survey of well over seven thousand youth, both non-church and church and came up with some astonishing results that merit attention.

Strommen discovered that church and non-church youth were alike in their response to common adolescent problems. In addition to discovering the similarity of political/social attitudes of church and non-church youth, he identified five common problem areas. The areas identified were *dating, lack of self-confidence, parental relationships, teacher/classroom relationships, academic problems and lack of self-confidence.* [7]

Developmental psychologist such as Erik Ericson have clearly identified the characteristics or marks of various age groups and the kinds of struggles that take place in the search for identity. Identity heads the list. In the transition from one's childhood image to that of adulthood, important things take place during the period of adolescence. The struggle for self-identity absorbs a great deal of energy during this period. The need to sort out the need for intimacy and discover independence also becomes crucial during this period.

That is why it is crucial to understand the importance and place of a theology of youth ministry. A solid theological foundation for Youth Ministry provides the assurance of a meaningful ministry program. Our youth have been labeled many names in our times, "disillusioned generation', "fatherless generation" 'Baby Busters," Generation X, etc. The very labels raises the issue of a need for a theology to address youth searching for meaning and identity in a society that sends mixed messages to them.

The same old Gospel must be couched in a new language that speaks to youth without minimizing their personhood. The theological claims we make must be grounded in Scripture. Jesus grew in wisdom, stature and favor with God and humankind. When youth are facing crucial decisions such as their life's purpose, life's mate and life's career, they need caring informed people to provide a meaningful word grounded in basic Christian experience and lifestyle.

> **Is Youth Ministry integrally related to the total plan of your church's vision?**

How Youth Ministry is structured in relationship to the total church's ministry is of vast importance. It is important that lines of accountability be established. When youth feel connected and accountable to the established church, they develop respect and learn responsibility. The church will feel compelled to underwrite a ministry within established parameters that is essentially connected. In some churches the temptation is great to take the Youth Ministry and form a church-within-a-church. The consequences can be disastrous for anyone who takes this approach to Youth Ministry.

Remember it takes time to build an effective Youth Ministry. Youth Ministry should not evolve from a 'what-do-you-want-to do" approach to youth. It presupposes that youth know essentially what is best for them. This question deals primarily with "wants" rather than "needs." a meaningful Youth ministry should build upon "needs." Once essential "needs' are identified among youth, and meaningful programs are designed, their interest will peak. When 'needs' are built foundationally on the present with a view toward the future, you can be assured that a meaningful future for youth Ministry will be enhanced.

There are few things more beautiful than a church filled with young people who are bent on purpose. Do not despair the harvest of blessings for you may be much closer than you think. Youth leaders must focus on strong interpersonal relationships. Youth is a time of intense exploration, curiosity and adventure. The hormones are intensely active driving youth toward action. Relevant Youth Ministry must be present to give content and purpose to such actions.

What about unchurched youth? As we move toward the millennia the African- American community finds itself caught in the grip of a morbid social pathology unrivaled in its history. Add to this the visible erosion of Civil Rights gains the attack by the "Right" on Affirmative Action, and the gradual loss of our traditional value system that fostered Black humanity for centuries as we witness a bold new in your face kind of racism (covert and overt) that fuels this current pathology. Nowhere is this assault envisioned with greater clarity than in the plight of the African-American male. The unenviable sociological distinction of being singled out as an *endangered species*[8] is the present diagnosis of the Black male. The Pharaohs of our times continue to engage in the process of genocide, marginalization, incarceration and violent decimation of the Black male seed at a rapid rate in a clandestine manner.

Homicide rates in 1991 for Black males were 72.5 per 100,000 nearly 8 times higher than for white males. Homicide is the second leading cause of death among black children. It is the leading cause of death among black youth 15- 24 and the second leading cause of death among Black males ages 25-44.[9]

Who are Generation Xers? In algebra, "X" is the unknown quantity. Why have our youth been labeled "the unknown generation"? Where are their parents? Can they become the "generation" known for its faith?

Terminology   **Baby Boomers**   Birth Years > 1946 to 1964 > (33 to 51)

         Baby Busters   Birth Years > 1965 to 1983 > (14 to 32)(X)

         (Children- ??) X   Birth Years > 1984 to 2002> (under 14)

Baby Boomers= the 76 million children just past WW II and the Korean War; labeled "war babies"   Baby Busters= labeled because the period from 1965 -1983 produced fewer babies (a birth bust)

Many young Blacks don't fit neatly into either of the generational archetypes. Many **Generation Xers** are for the most part children of **"Baby Busters"** who have been labeled "the disillusioned generation."[10] Some data suggests that the birth dates of Xers begins in the seventies to the present.

In 1995 Generation Xers numbered 79.4 million people, about 65 million of them young adults. It is predicted that the population of Generation X adults will continue to grow at an average rate of approximately 3.6 million each year, until the year 2,000. By the year 2,000, there will be 79.8 million adult Xers, ranging in age from nineteen to thirty-nine years.

Economics Consumer **Marketers know that** Xers are well traveled and are as likely to have purchased a car. Relative to their numbers, they buy more CDS, consume more fast food, smoke more cigarettes, drink more cola and more likely to prefer an imported car. As Xers grow older they are more likely to be a member of a health club, become major consumers of health and exercise and sports equipment and clothing for sports and leisure. According to most syndicated research, Xers represent a good market for cameras, for clothing, for most cosmetic products and for certain kinds of financial products. They use more creme rinses, gel, and mousse than Boomers do. They drink more beer and wine coolers and are the volume consumers of rum, tequila and vodka. They use more tooth paste, chew more gum, wear contact lenses more often and play more video games. They are unquestionably the market of the future. [11]

For African-Americans the statistics are grimmer for Xers. While the number of Black families with incomes above $50,000 has more than quadrupled since 1967, there are more harsh realities. Between 1967 and 1987, cities like N.Y., Detroit, Chicago and Philadelphia lost more than half of their manufacturing jobs to sun belt states in the South and far West. By 1988, one in four Black children lived below half the poverty level. More affluent Blacks fled the inner city leaving increased concentrations of poverty, crime and violence.

This harsh reality may account in part for the way Young Blacks have embraced Hip Hop rhetoric that attacks the system and have focused on acquiring materialism by any means necessary, as they highlight the failures of the post-integration era. Parents and Xers are frustrated by the inequality that has persisted and deepened long after the diminishing gains of the civil rights movement. Hip Hop culture is impatient, unwilling to defer gratification. The names are revealing: Naughty by Nature, Tha Dogg Pound, Niggas With Attitude. Greetings have passed from "brother" to "home boy" to the contentious term "nigga."

Vignette: 1. Ice Cube (calls himself a "seven-figga nigga") "The world is mine, nigga, back up/I gots to get mine before I act up. Nobody told me about the struggle, so I didn't know how to continue the struggle. I just got that you have to get yours and don't worry about nobody" He refers to the late

Rapper Tupac Amaru Shakur as "the realest nigga in a world full of fakes."
Vignette 2. Tupack Shakur "I ain't a killer but don't push me/ Revenge is like the sweetest joy next to getting sex. " [12]
Vignette 3. Some Hip Hop music glorify drugs, crime, disrespect, sexism, weapons, murder etc. Xers saw the so-called "American dream" become a nightmare as they confused "wants" and "needs" Many times their wants also became their "needs.

Spiritually Generation Xers are in search of identity, purpose and meaning for their lives. What is identity? Identity is the essence of a person, the inner character he or she displays. Lack of identity stems from our inability to make prudent choices about our self-definition and to establish proper priorities. If you don't know who you are anyone can define you. The skyrocketing rate of divorce among parents of **Xers** left many of them lost, insecure and in search of surrogate parents. TV has become the surrogate parent. This "video mentor" watched by the average American family nearly 50 hours per week teach our youth many things. From the " tube" they learn inappropriate ways to resolve conflicts (often violent methods), the degradation of human sexuality and the " excitement of a defamed and irreligious life style.

How does one explain the behavior of a teen-ager in Jonesboro, Arkansas and a small town in Pennsylvania going on a rampage and killing their teachers. In spite of the 1994 Gun-Free Schools Act which order school districts to expel for one year any student form K-school to 12 who brings a firearm to school, 6,100 were expelled in 1997. According to a U.S.A. Today brief, May 11, 1998 a 5 year old was arrested in Memphis for bringing a fully loaded .25 caliber semiautomatic pistol to school to kill his teacher for disciplining him with a "time out." The teacher Margie Foster confiscated the weapon and turned it over to authorities. The five- year old was charged with carrying a weapon but it was uncertain whether he would be prosecuted, because, "a five- year old is not capable of forming criminal intent" according to court Judge Kenneth Turner.

Because many **Xers** are unfulfilled in their search, suicides rates have escalated. According to one psychiatrist, "teens who commit suicide are not endeavoring to kill themselves, but to kill the hopelessness that is part and parcel of their daily existence." Emile Durkeim the French sociological theorist cites "normlessness" as a primary cause of suicide. **Generation Xers** are in search of substance and meaning. The fact that they are confused, aimless and misdirected is a key to their deeper yearnings. Being heirs of a morally bankrupt society **Xers** tend to reject an institutionalized so-called "blue eyed blonde Hollywood) Jesus. They are not strung out on religiosity. They want something to believe even if it means following a Jim Jones (Guyana) or Heavens Gate cult (San Diego) to final death. They are weary of cheap grace and shallow platitudes. They would rather see a sermon than to hear one.

Proverbs 22: 6 "Train up a child in the way he should go and when he is old, he will not depart from it." It seems the best place to begin is with parents. How can we change youth without impacting parents? Males who have never been told by their parents they are loved. Females who have never been positively affirmed by their parents. As an ethicist I am biased. To change the morbid social pathology that has impacted the African American community we must start with values. "Ethics is a study of what is in light of what ought to be" according to my doctoral mentor in ethics, Dr. Clinton Gardner at Emory University.

Stewardship Inventory: God does not Want Your Money

- **Have you critically examined and evaluated your theology of stewardship?**

Stewardship involves managing and sharing our total resources in a responsible and disciplined manner because we are blessed.

A foundational area that contributes to the well being and continuation of the church's ministry is stewardship. Many churches either fail to intelligently discuss it or spend too much time stressing stewardship in a negative way. People should never get the impression during the time of giving that it is now "begging time." I strongly suggest that new members receive instructions about stewardship responsibility during the orientation sessions. I have observed churches where new members are expected to participate in financial drives as soon as they join the church. This is a dangerous fatal practice for churches who need to effectively and meaningfully close their back door.

The primary task of theology is to clarify the nature of the Christian faith for the believing community. Churches must resolve the question, are members giving in order to be blessed or rather because they are blessed? Prosperity doctrine in our time has led to a great deal of confusion in the church. Prosperity doctrine starts with the premise that God desires that all of His children prosper. Proponents posit 1 John 3:1 (Beloved I would that thou mayest prosper and be in health even as thy soul prosper), as a guarantee of such a desire. From an exegetical point this passage is taken out of context and forced to say what it was not intended to state. This passage is a greeting and not a promise.

Prosperity proponents not only confuse desire and need, but they insult persons in other cultures where poverty is cultural. Will prosperity doctrine work for Christians in India and the Sahara where poverty is cultural? Even Paul admonished us that persons of corrupt minds destitute of the truth would appear, who would *"suppose that gain is godliness, from such withdraw."......But godliness with contentment.* (1 Timothy 6: 5-6v.)

Prosperity doctrine has made a profoundly popular appeal with a significant number of 'baby boomers" and "baby busters" who fit the profile of upwardly mobile social climbers. Many of them have never been hungry one day in their lives and do not have the slightest hint of what it means to struggle. We must be discerning and critically examine popular teachings that spring up over night. If the theological claim is faulty, it will not remain for long.

This doctrine eliminates any biblical claim that points to suffering. To radically follow Jesus means to "expect the unexpected." My mentoring friend for the long journey, Bishop O.T. Jones of Philadelphia preaches a sermon that stresses the fact that wherever we are headed, 'our middle name is Job." We may lose everything we own materially in one day. There is something meaningful about the assurance that regardless to what takes place around us, it is only occasional and has to do with circumstances. The fact that we have Cosmic backing assures us of a joy that can never be canceled. Theology is neither right or wrong, it is either good or bad, for it must stand the test of Scripture. Your theology of stewardship must be meaningfully grounded in Scripture in order to be fruitful and productive for ministry. God really wants you rather than your money. The key is to develop a one hundred percent tithing tithing church.

Can we improve God's status in the universe by what we give? What was at stake throughout the Old Testament as people gave special offerings and sacrifices to God? Was God merely satisfied with their burnt offerings or was something more expected? The freewill offerings we give in worship has its basis in the concept of sacrificial offerings prevalent in Old Testament times.

Sacrificial offerings were the means by which persons hoped to atone for their sins and restore fellowship with God. Such blood sacrifices were effective only when offered in faith in the promised sacrifice (Gen. 3:15; Heb. 9:8-9; 10:8-9, 16-17)

One such sacrificial offering was the Peace Offering. Known also as a heave offering and a wave offering, the Peace Offering was a bloody offering presented to God. Part of the offering was eaten by the priest (representing God's acceptance) and part was eaten by the worshiper and one's guest who could either be non-officiating priests, Levites and the poor. In this sense it could be stated that symbolically, God hosted the meal. This sacrifice celebrated covering of sin, forgiveness by God, and the restoration of a right relationship with God.

There were three kinds of peace offerings: 1) thank offerings in response to an unsolicited special divine blessing; 2) Vowed (votive) offerings were presented in pursuit of making a request or pledge to God; and 3) Freewill offerings spontaneously presented in worship and praise. It is the latter offering from which we derive our manner of giving today. In Exodus as a response to the Hebrews deliverance from Egyptian bondage, *"none shall appear before me empty."* God cannot be manipulated into blessing us at any time. He sends His blessings upon the unjust as well as the just. What God sends is one thing, the way we manage is another issue. The law of sowing and reaping is as real now as it ever has been.

Throughout the whole of Scripture the determining factor of one's lot was not how much they gave, but rather their attitude toward giving. That is the essence of stewardship. Recently this came home to me through a rather trying experience. In planning seminars I encourage churches to plan months in advance. I had scheduled a major seminar five months in advance with full confirmation. My verbal confirmation did not reach the administrative secretary through some error on the part of a secretary who had received my message. I received a letter of cancellation two days prior to my departure. It was the first time I had to endure this misery. Many clergy are financially out of control due to lack of a financial plan.[13]

It literally took me three weeks to recover both psychologically and fiscally. Needless to say it was a devastating experience as I faced the first of the month, having advanced credit toward the weekend. The church only made a verbal promise but did not respond in any other way. It took me three weeks of day-by-day crisis management to overcome this near disaster. It was a close call because I did not have the proper stewardship plan in place.

It took a Saturday morning call from my special friend Pastor Ricky Temple, of the **Overcoming Faith Foursquare Church** in Savannah, Georgia to lay it on the line.

There are some conversations we hold dear for a life time. I can still hear Ricky Temple saying, your present crisis has nothing to do with what you are receiving. It has to do with your attitude toward money. He went on to say that the countless number of counseling cases that he encounters weekly has roots in economic problems. I spent the rest of the day working on the most serious budget I have ever developed in my life. I started implementing it before the inaugural date. Ricky was really reminding me that I had been dealing with discipleship of one's spiritual life but had profoundly omitted one area that has literally destroyed individuals, families and churches.

For Reflection and Dialogue

1. Are you aware that when you evangelize various people groups in the city you are in effect evangelizing the world?

2. When was the last time your church seriously re-vamped its worship and music ministry in order to make it related and relevant?

3. Is your church really nurturing its people in a meaningfully way? Be specific and give examples in your response.

4. Does your church impose a "structured program" on its youth or does it develop from within with serious guidance?

Chapter

9 DISCOVERY: ITS THE BEST LOCK!

▸ **Why Bother Joining a Church?**

We were created for fellowship with other persons. Our very creatureliness demands that we live in relationship to other human beings. Many non-churched often ask whether one really need to join a church in order to be Christian. The question should be re-framed to ask, "would a person who becomes Christian not desire to unite with other Christians in worship"? While there are many distinctive fellowships in existence, the Christian Church is unique with a common loyalty to Christ which makes Christians one everywhere. A second unique feature of the Christian Church is that it is the bearer of the gospel of Jesus Christ. A third feature of the Christian Church is its call to make worship primary. In Hebrews 10:25 we are admonished to: *"Not forsaking the assembling of ourselves together, as the manner of some is; but exhorting one another; and so much the more, as ye see the day approaching"*.

The Christian Church transcends culture, ethnicity, class, racial and national origins and is therefore by its very nature able to unite diverse people groups. The universal nature of the Church makes real a hymn we sing:

> *In Christ there is no East or West,*
> *In Him no South or North;*
> *But one great fellowship of love*
> *Throughout the whole wide earth.*

The Christian Church as "the Body of Christ," to borrow a Pauline metaphor implies unity in diversity, and that such unity is made possible by the presence of the Spirit of Christ that makes a group of ordinary people a Church. According to Georgia Harkness, *"When we wish to stress the unity of the Church, which embraces in its fold the faithful of all ages, the living and the dead, we call it 'the communion of saints'.*[1] I appreciate E. Stanley Jones penetrating statement that, *"there is no real promise of hope from any direction except the Church of Jesus Christ, if that Church is truly Christian"* in *The Reconstruction of the Church*. Theologically the church as a spiritual organism cannot be managed in the same way as corporate America.

As a sociological institution the church may even borrow a few principles from the "children of this world". Since Jesus Christ is the Head of the spiritual "body" we recognize on earth as the church of the Lord, it is He who as Lord of the Church who must inform its true agenda. Doing the right thing and following all the right principles and methods will not assure us of guaranteed success in our ministry to persons. We must affirm at the outset that Jesus is Lord of the church and everything that we do must be properly aligned with that fact alone.

The great nineteenth century Evangelist Dwight L. Moody, was asked by someone why was it necessary for Christians to attend church. Instead of providing a direct answer to the question, the Evangelist reached into a fireplace and lifted a red-hot coal out of the fire and placed on the hearth, and walked out of the room. When he returned later, the coal was no longer burning. Separated from the other burning rubbish, the coal had gone out. Without saying one word, Dr. Moody had offered a life-changing response to the inquisitor. One of the many purposes of the church is to be present as a place of spiritual resource to build up each member in the body. In the "body of Christ' spiritual gifts are shared for the mutual benefit of each member present. To be absent from this exchange is not only to be deprived of what God will send, but to deprive others from receiving what God can share through you.

▸ **Should Orientation for New Members be Optional?**

Whether you are purchasing a car, computer or condominium, orientation of some kind utilizing definite instructions usually with a manual is necessary. A serious initial new member orientation ministry is a preventive measure for spiritual road hazards. Like a manual for new equipment you purchased, it saves you from 'pushing the wrong button'. Several years ago

Church of the Savior near Washington, D.C. had a mandatory two year new member orientation ministry that even included such items as a concentrated Bible study. One must ask why did this church maintain a waiting list. As a church with a special mission, calling and ministry in the world, they assigned a particular value to membership. There are certain exclusive private clubs that will accommodate special clientele. Prices and special services remain in a category that makes the club exclusive.

While the church must retain its voluntary character, it must also state clearly the goals and standards of the Kingdom of God. While the church is not the Kingdom, it is the foyer. One may be in the institutional church and not be in the Kingdom, but it is impossible to be in the Kingdom and not be in the invisible church. Orientation prepares new members for future pilgrimage in the church. Without it one could enter the institutional church and second-guess one's way through the various commitments and expectations that emanate from the 'body of Christ'. Orientation prepares the new member for a deeper commitment with the Lord by explaining the significance of one's faith and the meaning of Christian doctrines and symbols for the new believer. Orientation gives the new member a sense of ownership within the Community of faith where the barriers come down and Jesus is Lord of the church.

During my pastorate in Los Angeles at Crossroads Church, orientation was mandatory except membership transfer. For members transferring from our denomination, new member orientation was optional. I now believe in hindsight it should have been mandatory for all persons joining the fellowship. All churches (even within the same denomination) are different in philosophy, approach and life-style. The class for new members was called '**The New Life Class**'. Classes were intentionally held concurrent during the Sunday School hour in order to prepare the new member for future attendance in Sunday School. The Sunday School Superintendent must be passionately intentional in planning classes so as to direct new members to classes designed to meet their budding needs as babes in Christ.

Orientation class attempted to cover seven specialized areas during a seven week period. The areas were as follows:

- *Session One   History and Emergence of your Church and Ordinances*
- *Session Two   Humankind as Sinful*
- *Session Three The New Birth- Justification and Sanctification*
- *Session Four   The Baptism in the Holy Spirit*
- *Session Five   Stewardship- God does not want your Money*

- *Session Six   Victorious Living*
- Session Seven   *Sharing Your Faith   see Appendix for outline detail* *

    The orientation sessions were kept dialogical and taught in an inspirational manner. *Esprit de corps* was always high in those sessions. The Holy Spirit would visit those sessions in special ways that always defied our normal expectations. As a kind of discipline for future involvement, all new members were required to be on time. Discussions always extended beyond the assigned class time. As pastor I felt great pride in teaching this class. Over a period of time I noticed that ninety-five per cent of the persons who completed new member orientation remained with the church for the long journey. Likewise, those who did not complete orientation sessions drifted into a state of inactivity.

> **Indoctrination or Discipleship? Which shall it be?**

In order to effectively close the back door of your church there are certain essentials that are considered fundamental to the well-being of those who walk in the Christian vocation. In order to assure each believer of the blessed hope that is within them it is crucial that a serious ministry of discipleship takes place. One must be careful that indoctrination is not substituted for discipleship. Indoctrination utilizes force or undue pressure to implant certain values within individuals. A common term we use is "brainwashing". There are certain basic spiritual truths a new believer must know and apply to develop maturity and become grounded in the faith.

    Discipleship is a radical commitment to validating the conversion experience through following our Lord in every way. It involves the challenge of spiritually multiplying ourselves through others. Gary Kuhne calls this process "life transference." [2] Discipleship entails the result of conscious application of biblical principles, and not just coincidence. [3] It is a part of the Great Commission (*Matthew 28: 18 - 20*) *"to go into all the world and make disciples"* with the ultimate goal of reaching the world for Christ. Waylon B. Moore in his provocative book, **_Multiplying Disciples_** stated, *"When the church exhales disciples, it inhales converts".* [4]

    Nearly two decades ago, Juan Carlos Ortiz the renown pastor from Buenos Aires admonished us that if a church is growing numerically without discipling it is merely growing fat and the result is the eternal childhood of believers. That pastors are not to *entertain or maintain believers, but to mature them.*[5] The goal for Paul was to present every believer perfect (mature) in Jesus Christ. That process should begin during orientation and continue beyond that initial beginning so believers can graduate from the ABC's of the faith.

When the technique of indoctrination is used within the church, mechanical robots are produced. Persons are produced who are enslaved by rules and the ruler. The yoke of Jesus is a lifting yoke for believers. Jesus used persuasion rather than force as He spoke as *'One having authority".* Love is the norm for the Kingdom of our Lord, and His followers respond out of reverence and not fear. We are drawn to Jesus through a love that will not let us go. There is no room for iron-fisted force and mean spiritedness in His Kingdom. Indoctrination or discipleship, which shall it be? Discipling new believers so that they will reproduce themselves in others is the challenging goal and yet it is the road to spiritual maturity. We must move beyond the ABC's of the faith to the hidden wisdom of the ages and on to the mystery of godliness as we bask in the sunlight of His glory.

The Adoption Plan:Transitioning to a New Environment

This is the beginning of an exciting venture for the new believer in Christ. New believers should be told with excitement and enthusiasm that they are now part of the army of God. That His Kingdom is beyond military might. Since they are now a part of the new creation in Christ Jesus, they are very special. On the other hand a great deal of care should be taken as though you are dealing with *"new born babes who desire the sincere milk of the word."*(1 Cor.3:) During this period of transition for newcomers, older members can make this a time of celebration and wonder. New members should be welcomed as a new link in a chain of believers who through the centuries have trusted God and accepted Jesus as Lord of their life.

We must remember that many who accept Christ have evolved from a setting that has provided them with a variety of life-styles and experiences. They must indeed be prepared for their new walk with Christ. When Jesus spoke of coming to Him as "little children," that challenge alone inspires the imagination. Little children are excited by new things, as they live on the edge of wonder. New members should be told that they are entering the environs of the Kingdom. Their very presence will impact the world as they are impacted by the power of the Kingdom. The first disciples of Jesus followed our Lord with a great deal of excitement and wonder. They brought their full humanity to the task. Hence Simon Peter came with his tempestuous character and fiery, raging temper. Andrew came with his knack for reliability. James the Zealot came with his spirit of militancy. **Others came** with their unique humanity and placed themselves at the feet of the Master. The only thing they did was change masters. Their unique abilities were re-energized, re-focused and re-directed. They were now to become fishers of persons. They were now followers of the Lamb who would eventually overcome the lion in history. New Christians should also be informed that they will be challenged in many ways to give up their faith. The very challenges they overcame in order to walk with the Lord will rise up to challenge them along the way. Drugs, gang warfare, prostitution, crime, social and economic dislocation, dysfunctional relationships, apathy, psychic destruction have left their mark on this "disillusioned' generation. The church must remain vigilant as it participates with new believers in their transition to a new life in Christ. Our generation is the last generation that will remain in the church out of sheer family loyalty.

We must be vigilant in teaching "sound doctrine that cannot be condemned' if we are to prevail as the representative of our Lord on earth. According to Jesus, new wine will burst old wineskin. Today, we must reassess the foundational first principles we transmit to new believers entering a new environment. Introducing new believers to an appreciation of the word of God can be an exciting adventure for new members who indeed should be challenged to become Kingdom disciples in a world moving toward judgment and destruction.

There is a sense in which new members are like new infants who need special care until thy can stand alone. To assist new members in transitioning to their new spiritual environment we suggest spiritual adoption. Every precaution must be taken in making sure the spiritual environment for the new believer is secure. In this case adoption is a temporary measure on the part of matured believers as they enter into a special relationship with new members. Such a relationship is crucial for spiritual development.

I would suggest that a tracking system be set up and implemented in an efficient manner. New members should be identified according to the geographical zone of the city that they reside. A matured member of the same sex living in proximity to the new member should be assigned the responsibility of monitoring their involvement in the life of the church for at least three months. It would mean making sure the person assigned attends mid-week service and of course the Sunday service and meet special commitments that are expected.

The adoption ministry should be directed by an Adoptions Coordinator who can work effectively with a pastoral staff member in assigning new members to matured Christians for special oversight. The success or failure of this specialized ministry rest squarely on the shoulders of every member who accepts an adoptions assignment. Since we are children of God by a special new birth, we should rejoice that we can participate as enablers of new believers in the Kingdom transitioning to the Community of Faith.

The new member adoptions ministry can be an effective tool in monitoring new comers. It can be an effective tool for communicating the message that we are concerned about your spiritual development and maturity from the time you arrive. We will not give up on you as we share the very life of God. We are intentional in forming special ministry partnerships for the long journey. We are also intentional in providing a special ministry of nurture as you embark upon your spiritual pilgrimage with us. We are your extended family. We are your new brothers and sisters in the Lord and you can depend upon us. Many will come and go but you are special. In essence, we are here for you in authentic ministry. When such a message is communicated in deed, it is difficult for new members to just abandon the fellowship. Persons performing leadership tasks in this area must be willing to exercise patience. One must be willing to absorb the fall out that new people bring to the table. It has been done and it can be done effectively.

- **Communion with God: Just Keep on Praying**

Prayer at its deepest level is communion with God. Prayer is to the Christian life what fuel is to engines. It energizes believers for struggling, coping and living a full and rewarding life. E. Stanley Jones reminds us that *"prayer rewinds the springs of life."* In his now classic book ***The Way*** Jones remarks that someone has defined prayer: *"To bring the whole of life into the light of God's presence for cleansing and decision---that is prayer."* It is also power. For in prayer we align our will with God's will. Living life is no longer a burden.[6]

The late George Buttricks, relates a moving story about prayer from E. Herman account of "The Nun of Lyons." She was dancing at a fashionable ball. None was gayer or lovelier: her marriage to the most eligible man of her set was due within a week. Suddenly, in the midst of a minuet, she saw the vision of the world dying--for lack of prayer, She could almost hear the world's gasping, as a drowning man gasps for air. The dance now seemed macabre, a dance of dance. In the corner a priest, smiling and satisfied discussed the eligibles with a matchmaking mother: even the Church did not know that the world was dying--for want of prayer. As instant as a leaping altar flame she vowed her life to ceaseless intercession, and none could dissuade her. She founded a contemplative order of prayer---lest the world should die. Was she quite wrong? Was she wrong at all? Or is our world saved by those who keep the windows open on another world?

In prayer we discover God. We may never know the "why" of our circumstances. God's grace may not take the form of a specific answer to our questioning. In communion with God we discover something more important than our specific question. We discover God anew. In that important event we discover anew that life has special meaning and significance. Surprising and wonderful things happen when we commune with God. The touch of God transforms us from what we are to what we are meant to be in the intention of God. Where God abides, wonderful things happen.

Communion with God enhances our inner journey. We must learn to walk in our own path all the way to the throne of God. At the mercy seat we journey with God to the depths and core of our inner life. Specific times with God brings caution and growth at the point of need, for us, not at the point of desires. We are proned by nature to drift to the familiar and comfortable, rather than confront truth and change. When we truly commune with God we nail down the deep, genuine and real needs of our life. We are really inviting confrontation with radical truth and change. When you commune with God you can pinpoint your real need with an openness to God's response despite any pain involved in the encounter.

Whatever God does you will discover that it will be right and better for you in the long journey. The deepest prayer of our heart should be that we know how to pray and to know that for which we should pray. All things that we encounter may not be good for us, but as we commune with God we can be assured that they are working for our good. (Romans 8:28) The judgments of the Lord are righteous, and the truth of that reality alone should satisfy those who wonder. To dwell in God's presence is the "source of our security." God will be God, and that is the foundation for our hope.

This significant gathering has come to be a central feature in the spiritual life of this congregation and has brought renewal to this church. Several churches across the nation have modeled this period designated for communion with God. When people are personally encouraged from week to week in the midst of difficult times, they will remain with a church.

Authentic spirituality is one of the sure elements in closing the back door of any church. It is the genuine and real that stabilizes a congregation.

▸ Communicating with Others: Keep on Talking

Whenever people keep communicating they will usually find the right answers to life's most perplexing questions. Have you ever wondered why marriage counselors spend a great deal of time on the issue of communication? Therapist know that many marriages including Christian ones falter and dissipate because the partners do not communicate with each other. Communication is a skill that is learned. It is so important that we are reminded that the process of communication feeds a relationship. That the actual *experience* of communicating is as significant as the words that are spoken. [7] The church like a marriage requires regular and adequate nourishment.

In communication theory we learn that "the way a message is stated is as important in most instances as the message itself." That is why good communicators give significant thought to not only the words chosen, but also to the tone of voice, physical gestures, body language and other nonverbal tools. Timing and the use of silence are important abstract factors that are crucial in communication. Finding the "right" moment to say a particular thing may be as important as the message you would like to convey. Silence can be utilized as a powerful tool in communication.

When fists are clenched, arms and legs tightly crossed, the body is rigid as lips are pursed, you can conclude that you are in the presence of a defensive person even though no words have been spoken. Your body movements, facial expressions, and gestures reveal much more about your attitudes and emotional state than your words.[8]

Within the context of the church, *"if one person communicates all the time, while the others only listen, this sense of fellowship will suffer."* On the other hand, *'if the communicative roles of source and receiver, of information giver and asker, of problem definer and solution-giver, and all the other functions of communication are exchanged, a greater sense of fellowship and groupness will result."* [9] Congregations tend to bond firmly in the presence of good communication. One should strive against possible odds to develop a ministry fellowship where members learn to keep on communicating. It will be a source of encouragement to those who are new in the fellowship and for those who have been with the church for a while. When we learn to "speak to" each other rather than" talk at" each other, we are well on the way toward closing the back door of the church.

As a pastor I have observed new members leave the ministry due to either lack of communication, poor communication or frustration generated by controlling members who deliberately clearly communicated the wrong message. *Can the* church present a strong witness when conflict separates members due to poor communication? When we respectively communicate to each other, many positive rewards can result. Information exchange, conflict resolution, behavior modification and problem solving can take place when we engage in the act of simple communication. Every pastoral leader should seek to facilitate free flowing and easily understood communication within the ministry fellowship.

Values, attitudes, beliefs and behavior are changed through the process of communication. Sometimes groups are formed for the purpose of modifying one members behavior. Communication is the bearer of people's attempt to actually change the behavior of others.[10] For persons to mature within the environment of the sacred, they must feel safe in expressing their ideas or opinion whether they are right or wrong.

In conflict resolution within the ministry fellowship it may be necessary to focus on the problem rather than on specific solutions. Sometimes it may be necessary to use the communication strategy of confrontation to break through a communication barrier. When confrontation is utilized as a strategy it must be done skillfully or it can escalate the very conflict one seeks to resolve.[11] As followers of our Lord we are obliged to strive for peace not at the expense of justice. The peace we seek is "Shalom" that is inclusive of justice grounded in agape love.

Chapter

10 Passion: Closing the Back Door Permanently

▸ **Let's Try Scratching where People are Itching**

A church will increase to the extent the needs of its constituents are being met. Every church either consciously or unconsciously crafts and channels the gospel message in creative ways that reflect its own ministry style. One can also find rich messages in a church's "hidden curriculum." This is composed of the values, beliefs, language and lifestyle developed over the years. A church's functional message will rub off on you as you encounter its members who are under spiritual discipline.

We must ask, are we "scratching" where our people are "itching?" America is a diverse nation. We have learned how to co-exist with many institutions that are different and sometimes diametrically opposed to what we espouse. Currently the non-traditional, less formal church fellowships appear to be making massive appeal. What are these non-traditional fellowships doing? They are attempting to address the needs of people in transition. Our society has become transient. Many families do not remain in one place for more than seven years. A church must be prepared to address the problem of rootlessness which is at the root of our present cultural crisis. At this juncture in history it appears that every opportunity has not only the potential for danger but also holds more opportunity.

The present era for this planet will not be "business as usual' politically, economically, socially or personally. With exciting changes occurring rapidly across the earth, comes new challenges. The recent upsurge in domestic terrorism has fostered a deep insecurity. This is indeed an era of distinct significance for the Kingdom of God. Non-traditional fellowships appear to have the flexibility to effect high tolerance for mobile rootless people in search of meaning.

Churches must find a way to gear its ministry in such a way that it provides a sense of security and purpose for those who worship. Our youth must be given directives that are life changinging and grounded in spirituality. We are living in a society saturated with sex. One cannot watch public TV and not be affected by its emphasis on sexuality. Youth need a sound frame of reference in which to make concrete decisions. Discovering the rich meaning of the symbols of one's faith is crucial for youth who are in the process of physical and spiritual maturation. As the "twig is bent' so will it grow.

Youth need a sound frame of reference in which to make concrete decisions....in order to keep it real!

New experiences and ways of thinking lead naturally to new ways of living and acting. Authentic ministry requires presence, but such presence must be more than just a preaching presence, it must include empowerment. The church is not a welfare station, it is at its radical best a power center. It must also provide a new self-understanding for people with a distorted understanding of who they really are. To say the church should posture itself to "scratch" where people are "itching" is not a call for a kind of theological narcissism. We must proceed with caution and make sure that we do not compromise the very Gospel we proclaim by providing a "spiritual" comfort zone within the church that reduces our message to nothing more than polished high level marketing. Should user-friendliness be the norm rather than a commitment to fearlessly proclaiming the whole counsel of God without weighing the consequences.

The attempt to accommodate the entire constituency of a traditional church is a major task. The process must not be so controlled that one experiences a loss of freedom at the expense of commitment to traditional values that have proven to be valuable over a period of time. The fundamental issue is whether one can employ a market-driven strategy in order to accommodate the faithful and remain faithful to Scripture? Our primary task is that of meeting the spiritual needs of those who constitute the Community of Faith. We are called to the task of creating community where authentic fellowship has primacy. Entertainment cannot be our primary goal as we engage in the process of enriching and deepening the life of those who love God on behalf of the Kingdom

We must be strategic and intentional when it comes to facing the challenges and meeting the "spiritual" needs of those to whom we minister. Elsewhere it has been said that the fundamental goal for believers is maturity. True Christian maturity cannot be measured simply on what a person knows, but rather in terms of one's life-style. It would be a travesty of great proportions if churches spent their resources in attempting to bring the world to the church rather than taking the church into the world. Strategic in the sense that we recognize that our task is to prepare those to whom we minister for the task of participating with God in the reconciliation of the lost, estranged and alienated. Intentional in the sense that participation with God requires a certain kind of discipline, witness and focus. As Christians we are called not only to believe but also to belong. We must be prepared to act out of commitment, vision, obedience, covenant and passion. The nurturing of each of these is a process and a process presupposes a time line.

Developing and Cultivating Interpersonal Relationships

The Double-Bolt Lock: Interpersonal Relationships

Karen Horney in her book *The Neurotic Personality of Our Time* describes in a rather unique way the dynamics behind our two driving passions. The first is our compulsion to be loved, often expressed in extreme sexuality and secondly, our quest for power, neurotically expressed in a passionate competitiveness. These are in fact the symptoms of our deep rooted anxiety. One must admit that there is glaring truth in Horney's statement when we view the over emphasis on sexuality and the quest for power, success, recognition and material gain in our time. It was into such a culture that the early church was born.

Indeed we are products of an urbane culture. Ours is a sensate culture according to the late famed sociologist, Pitirim Sorokin who compared the Roman world, into which the early church was born, with our society in his often quoted book *The Crisis of Our Age.* The writings of other sociologist such as Robert Park, George Simmel and Louis Wirth, among others, focus on a number of characteristics presumed to be the casual consequences of urbaneness. As the world becomes increasingly urban it can be postulated that the following also increases:

1. Increasing complexity of the division of labor and system of social stratification
2. Territorial and social mobility
3. Participation in voluntary interest groups or associations
4. Spatial segregation
5. Functional interdependence
6. Normative Deviance
7. The toleration of social differences
8. The degree to which behavior is controlled by indirect means.
9. Personal anonymity in interpersonal contacts [1]

In order to place a double-bolt lock on the backdoor of your church it is crucial that you understand the necessity of comprehending interpersonal relationships within the context of today's church. Books on pop psychology that points to quick fixes about self-understanding are on best sellers lists all over North America. The demand for the services of psychiatrists and mental health specialists also points to the urgency with which people are seeking self-understanding. We are preoccupied with such questions as "what makes us behave as we do?" "What really drives our behavior?" "How do we explain our compulsive behavior?" One cannot realistically relate to other apart from relating to oneself. A distorted view of one's self-worth and self-acceptance impacts negatively our view of others.

Pastoral leaders would do well to seek training in pastoral care that would enhance their interpersonal skills. We are attempting to minister to persons who are invariably related or are a part of a family. May times they are from troubled families. As human beings we are created in such a way that we tend to act out of a desire to fulfill inner needs. Those who cannot effectively bring their desires under discipline can also become victimized by same. When needs are met, desire diminishes.

These fundamental human needs can be classified as physiological, affiliative and status. Physiological need entails such needs as sleep, food, drink and sexuality. Affiliative needs embrace such needs as the need to love and reciprocate same, to give and reciprocate affection, companionship, understanding and sympathy. These needs cause us to form interpersonal and interdependent relationships with others. Status needs entail the need for recognition, appreciation, acceptance, self-esteem and fulfillment. All of our needs are God-given and are uniquely ours.[2]

Pastoral leaders who become adept at building interpersonal relationships within the confines of the church will in time develop a strong formidable ministry. As a spiritual community the church is also a social institution. An institution is *a set of norms governing a specific form of socially organized activity or behavior in group situations.* Institutions are normatively crystallized ways of acting.[3] The group is *an organized aggregate of persons in interaction.* The city is *a place where new institutions often are formed and where deviant institutions exist precariously particularly where cities are undergoing rapid urbanization.* Rapidity of social change impacts the structures of groups and their activities and functions.

Whenever two or more persons interact with each other within the Community of Faith the dynamic of interpersonal relations is present. Sometimes these relationships may be stable, mutually supportive and characterized by clear communications. There are times when such relationships are marked by persistent conflict. How persons get along with each other within the Community of Faith should be the primary concern of the pastoral leader. Paul the Apostle mentioned the need to give attention to such interpersonal tensions as strife, jealousy, anger, temper, slander, gossip, disputes and other issues that fall within the parameters of interpersonal relationships.

When a pastoral leader comprehends the nature of conflict within the context of the local parish the need for counseling is reduced. The goal in counseling is to assist persons to look within themselves to find handles in the resolution of inner conflict. However interpersonal skills are much more effective when the counselor operates through the medium of love and acceptance. Human beings are incredibly complex creatures. It is a blessing when skilled pastoral leaders can intervene in such a way so as to minimize conflict, prevent interpersonal tension and assist parishioners in avoiding self-destructive behaviors.

Ministries that are people-centered tend to thrive in contrast with those who are not focused on same. Thriving churches usually love and loving churches usually expand. A church should be Christocentric in nature but people-centered in fellowship. In such a church people are led not driven. In such a church people are assigned priority over property. After the descent of the Holy Spirit on the Day of Pentecost recorded in the Acts of the Apostles, social concerns and fellowship was given primacy. Young believers went from house to house breaking bread and enjoying authentic fellowship. The early church grew by leaps and bounds. Special persons were assigned to take care of tables, while others gave themselves to prayer and the ministry of the word.

Five decades ago, Gordon Cosby, former U.S. Chaplain founded the ecumenical and interracial Church of the Savior in Washington, D.C. with thirty dollars and nine people. This unconventional church thrived because it was focused and people- centered. Two decades after its founding the membership was not large but was highly influential due to the influence it had exerted through mission, witness and ministry in the city. New member prospects had to complete two years of specialized studies to complete membership requirements. Everyone was considered to be a minister . The Church of the Savior later founded a ministry to the unchurched called the

Potter's House. It was a coffee house ministry built around conversation. Artist, writers, poets business persons, scientist would gather to debate issues of Christian concern, significant conversation and to hear readings and see art exhibits. The Potter's House operated a unit Workshop where staff intentionally sought to reintegrate Christianity and the creative arts. Church members and strangers could take courses that sought to relate Christian faith to the arts and in so doing the fellowship was making one statement to the city. *"We will serve you, we will be with you in the way in which you naturally gather. We are not afraid of you. You can come and see those strange people called Christians in the market place----not in their places of worship but in your own natural habitat. You can come and ask your questions. You can come and vent your hostilities. We will be with you six nights a week. We will serve you, we will love you, we will pray for you..........We will just be there where you can find us "*[4]

That is the basic function of the church, to just "be there" where people can find it and be found. The Church of the Savior purchased a huge farm in the country hillsides of Maryland to be used as a retreat. The power of its ministry is its ability to be visible in the lives of its members and within the community without announcements. The Church of Jesus Christ "is" what it "does." In today's environment the opportunity to build a people-centered church is unlimited. We live in a society that is suffering for lack of authentic community. A people-centered church can be the basis for authentic community without becoming narcissic and self-centered.

People-centered churches intentionally attempt to make membership genuine rather than nominal. The church must never be confined to a particular plot of ground.. The church should be where its members are functioning in ministry. Effective ministry is contagious. Such contagion spreads and spreads within the community as well as existing organizations. Effective ministry constitutes the original and not the copy. Churches encrusted with tradition and weighted down with the burden of church trappings usually do not qualify for effective ministry, for they are too caught up and entangled with their own brand of "introverted institutionalism" (the church engaged in conversation with itself).

▶   **Its Way Past Time to Free the Sisters**

For three decades America has witnessed two great human revolutions. One was that of the Black Revolution with its stress on pride and militancy. The other has been the rising demand by women from their pre-defined roles in a male-dominated society. White feminist thought often excluded Blacks and others from the debate. More recently Black women have entered the debate in such areas as racism in education, politics, sexuality, male/female relationships and their share in all aspects of society including ministry. My goal is not to enter into a lengthy debate, but to stress the point that there is a freedom in Jesus Christ that liberates us from all the bondages and fetters of class, race, and gender.

The fundamental issue is not whether God can use women in ministry, but rather to what extent are they being used. We really need to redefine ministry for the twenty first century. When God pours out His Spirit upon all flesh it is an inclusive divine action. How can one deny the presence and sanction of God upon women who conduct major ministries in our times. I have had the opportunity to share with such women as Bishop Audrey Bronson, **Open Door Sanctuary Church** in Philadelphia; Bishop Barbara Amos, **Faith Deliverance Center**, Norfolk, Virginia; Pastor Allene Gilmore, Gilmore Temple COGIC, Paterson, New Jersey; Pastor Michele White, Faith Temple, Bronx, N.Y.;Pastor Ernestine Rheems,Center of Hope Evangelistic Church, Oakland, California; Pastor Emma Creamer, **Cathedral of Fresh Fire**, Wilmington, Delaware; Pastor Wanda Davis Turner, CEO, **World Won for Christ, Inc.**, Inglewood, California. The list and many ministries goes on and on.

The fundamental issue is not whether God can use women in ministry, but rather to what extent are they being used

The God who used a Harriet Tubman to deliver over four hundred slaves by way of the Underground Railroad has not changed. God implements His will through those who are open and willing to be used by Him. God forbid that we posture ourselves in such a way that we deny persons from being who they perceive God has called them to be. The term minister in the New Testament was not culturally or gender bound. Our contemporary corruption of the term has left us operating in one dimensional strait jackets. During the period of the early church the term minister was used as a verb, an action word. There is a sense in which all Christians in the early church had a ministry of actively, dutifully, functionally and effectively working for God. Anyone who performed normal Christian functions was considered a minister. Helping widows, praying for the sick, exhorting the saints, leading others to Christ were all functions Christians performed. In the twentieth century the term minister is treated grammatically as a noun, the name of a person and theologically a position for one high status individual.

Over two decades ago two powerful events took place within the Black community. The first event was that of burgeoning Black pride and militancy particularly within the African-American community and persons of color globally. The second event was that of the demand by women for liberation from their slave postured roles in a male dominated society. With the rise of militant feminism came the need for definition. Women no longer felt the need to be relegated to the role of housewife. For some it was either/or. For others it was both/and. The latter group of females chose to contribute to family life as a housewife while at the same time exercising the option of selecting an alternative career.

It is known that certain segments of the feminist movement had been under attack for their selective wooing of women of color. Yet during the episode of the Clarence Thomas/Anita Hill hearings many feminist raced toward Hill with impressive speed to support what had appealed to them as rather galvanizing testimony. Debate, dialogue and discussion emerged with new vigor and candor between previously unaligned groups about the meaning of the treatment of women in this society and particularly those who complain of sexual harassment of any kind. Much speculation arose as to why Hill came forward. No single event since the Watergate event had created and generated such national debate. Only the O.J. Simpson murder trial exceeded the Thomas/Hill debacle in intense media coverage. Our nation and particularly the African-American community focused on race, gender, sexuality and intra-racial politics with a vitality never before engendered. Sexual politics in America would be changed forever.

Astute politicians were asking whether this was an in house deal by Democrats at the eleventh hour to embarrass the "good old boys club" of the Republican Party? Black males were asking whether this was a concocted ploy of revenge and retaliation toward Thomas by Hill for his malady of what she perceived to be "jungle fever" (jungle fever is the code name taken from Spike Lee's film of the same name, as an apt description for a black male's desire to sleep with a white woman)? Black women were speculating as to whether the Thomas/Hill scenario would exacerbate the ever present tensions they experience when rejected by Black males who have been lured by a white standard of beauty that few sisters even wish to emulate. For the first time sisters began to come forth with all kinds of sordid detail about the kind of sexism they had been exposed to both by white and Black males.

With the gift of freedom comes responsibility. Within the community of faith women must be trusted with the call of God upon their lives. Few churches are thriving churches where women are in bondage. The chemistry is off when a church is male dominated. As a pastor I discovered that our church began to progress in a different way once the trustee board was reconfigured to include women. Women brought unique insights to major tasks without a great deal of fanfare. As a community we learned that it was way past time to simply free the sisters.

► Create a Place for Men

When men come to Christ they should be assigned priority in making their transition from the street to the house of God. Churches that invest in men have the potential to become giants for God. The worst statement that can be made about new male converts is that we cannot find a place in the church for same. Single family households are still in need of mentoring role models for young males. Men are expected to be leaders of family life and the family constitutes a basic unit of society. The male ego is far different than that of a female.

No one can visit a modern prison and leave feeling normal. There is something wrong with a society that builds more prisons than classrooms. Unfortunately, the largest number of persons in our prisons are invariably people of color. The church must insist on asking why is this so? What is the threat posed to the future of society by this over emphasis on order often at the expense justice. Has justice become so color coded in our present society that is has come to mean "just us" and not them? The deadly consequences are startlingly obvious. There are more Black males in prison than in college, a sweeping indictment of a nation where justice is supposed to be color blind and not color coded.

The concern for lack of male involvement particularly within the African-American church becomes a grave issue when we learn from social analyst that social indicators for young Black males has deteriorated since 1960. [5]

That the problems of young Black inner-city males are so severe that society simply ignore them, isolate them in ghettos or simply put them out of sight. Urban welfare plantations have replaced the rural slave plantations. Unemployment and lack of education have exacerbated the crisis in a society that rewards hard work, productivity and competence. We must find a way to provide purpose to those who have become victimized.

The church must focus on the conditions that demean persons and rob them of their humanity. In certain African societies young men are assigned a prescribed set of duties that will aid in their transition from adolescence to manhood. Such duties may include hunting and preparation of food which demonstrates the ability to be a provider. A ceremony is held signifying passage into manhood. We must reverse the meaning of what constitutes manhood in our time. Manhood is not the ability to father a child, but rather the maturity to take responsibility for same.

Church leaders who deal with males need to remember that men tend to respond positively to respect and fairness. It may be that the church in our time may provide the key to the salvation of men who have not found authentic meaning in life. Men tend to be motivated by challenges. As a parent of four sons it is difficult to maintain a posture of dispassionate objectivity in addressing the issue of male involvement and their ultimate salvation. We know that a Generation of black males have been classified as endangered due to the presence of deviance and dysfunction that characterize their lives. The church must take on the role of a crisis intervener if this process of the demeaning and deprivation of the basic essentials of life and the right to be fully human is to be discontinued.

The church must find a way to be central to the concerns of those who suffer from such pain. I was impressed with the conduct of men at **Union Temple Baptist Church** located in the Anacostia section of southeast Washington in the District of Columbia. Pastor Willie Wilson sends a strong intense message to Black males who are a part of his ministry. While a strong exponent of Afrocentric worship, a strong emphasis is placed on achieving manhood and the struggle for survival. To be a man in Christ is to fulfill the calling to which God has intended. (See 2 Corinthian 12:) To create a place for men one must be willing to listen to the voice of God with serious intensity.

Mobilization: Unleashing Our Potential

Pastoral leaders must be intentional and deliberate about developing a church where every member is involved. Jerry Falwell built a mega-church in Lynchburg, Virginia by utilizing the principle of saturation----reaching every available person, by every available means, at every available time. His follow up method is equally aggressive. He utilizes several hundred group captains who maintain contact with the several thousand Sunday School attendees and track them by utilizing strictly maintained attendance records with appropriate follow up. Falwell has made significant use of the mass media in developing and maintaining the involved Thomas Road Baptist Church.[6]

For members to become totally involved is not something that naturally evolves because your church of brick and mortar occupies a particular space. Certain ingredients must be present in order to develop a totally involved church. Leadership must be shared. New Testament churches are administered by the principle of shared leadership. A congregation does not merely meet to transact official business. The goal is to discover and follow God's will for the group. One does not seek to muster "enough votes to win" on a particular issue and close the case. The corporate discovery of God's purpose for the local fellowship becomes the driving force for a totally involved church.

Churches who are totally involved usually exemplify strong characteristics of group identity. We are basically social beings with the need to belong. We live in a society of joiners. People join teams, clubs and other social groups in order to realize their somebodiness. What motivates persons is the feeling that they are part of a group that give meaning. I read of a high school coach who was extremely harsh to his players. Before the season was in full gear nearly half the team quit in deep despair. Within months most of the boys without exception ended up on drugs...When asked the reason for taking drugs, admitted that being on the team gave them special meaning. They really felt like somebody. When they quit the team suddenly they did not belong. It was not drugs these teens were seeking. They wanted to experience a sense of belonging that only the group provided.

Churches that are totally involved usually share strong spiritual moorings. A "prayer-share" group can provide the foundation for increasing deep spirituality. Such a group may convene weekly to study a biblical passage or a book on prayer, share personal and special needs and spend the rest of the time interceding. Such gatherings tend to galvanize parishioners. One can sense the presence of a fresh anointing when individuals have been in the presence of God for cleansing and decision-making. It is possible that emotional and physical healing can take place in settings where prayer takes place at a significant level.

In churches where members are totally involved, personal crises are processed and more easily confronted with the support of a genuine Christian fellowship. Life can often present us with brutal and crushing crises often without warning. Caring clusters can often provide the basis for touching special need areas in the lives of those who live with physical, emotional and psychic pain. Churches that are totally involved are usually inspired by visionary driven leaders whose aspirations tends to galvanize the group. In the New Testament the Kingdom of God was the foci around which the followers of Jesus placed their ultimate loyalties. When the Kingdom of God is central to the life of a congregation, the result is a people who are totally involved in God's plan for humanizing the world.

▸ **Unity: We are in this Together**

When the social, psychological and spiritual glue that holds people together is in place you can be assured that this is an essential component of *closing the back door of your church*. Unity is the key to broadening the influence of a totally involved church. Cooperation is the essential ingredient for congregational *unity*. When goals have been clearly defined and purpose has been clarified *unity* is the outcome. Somewhere I read that the wilful cooperation of snowflakes can bring a city to a grinding halt. When snowflakes cooperates, armies can be slowed down. Giant projects must go on hold when snowflakes get together.

I have observed football teams that had been completely shut out during the first half of a game go to the locker room and unite. I have watched such teams win. I have watched couples struggle in their marriage and in the midst of their crisis decide that barring a miracle they would not survive. Such couples become intentional about remaining together and unite around a common goal. Have you ever watched a parade? When marchers are out of step it is an unseemly sight. I recently observed the United States Marine Band perform at the U.S. Air Arena near the nation's capitol. The beauty and symmetry of each member was incredible. One could discern that this kind of performance was the result of many years of preparation and experience. They were indeed united!

Psalm 133 is a biblical reminder of the meaning of *unity*. That *unity* is pleasant and good. When the world views a united church they feel predisposed to join. Churches should become intentional about scheduling group activities that promote cooperation. *Unity* in Christ should be demonstrated in word and deed. The Apostle Paul addressed the issue of *unity* in 1 Corinthian 12:12 ff. *...For as the body is one, and hath many members, and all the members of that one body, being many, are one body; so also is Christ."* The body functions in an interdependent relationship to its parts.

When people decide to become responsible for the well being of others within the fellowship, a healthy atmosphere is created. When the atmosphere of a church exudes unity, new people are predisposed to remain. I have observed churches where it was quite obvious that the visible unity had been disturbed. Usually such disunity is the direct result of internal fighting, conflict and the thrust for power. I have observed major ministries fold due to failure to resolve internal conflict. Conflict in and of itself is neutral. The way we manage conflict is decisive in terms of on going relationships.

The church in our times has been likened to a passenger ship in the middle of the ocean. The ship strikes an iceberg that leaves a gaping hole in the bow. Passengers are not preoccupied with the class they have been assigned, survival is at stake. First class passengers will cooperate with second class passengers in order to work on this gaping hole. If proper attention is not given to the immediate crisis, passenger classification will not matter, survival is at stake. To work on a gaping hole that could result in the destruction of the ship requires united effort on the part of all persons on board.

The message of *unity* must resound through the entire Community of Faith that we are in this together. That everyone's destiny is interrelated to that of each other. No one can reach their ultimate destiny apart from that of the other. Such linkage is a derivative of their faith combined with spirituality. Such spiritual glue constitutes the making of a strong and determined church united to contend with forces that assailed community. Only a *united* church can deal with the pervasive ills and insanity that plague our community.

Only a united church can effectively deal with the pervasive ills and insanity that plague our community

Only a *united* church can effectively instill values that mean the difference between life and death for those to whom we must be responsible who remain immature and callous. Such *unity* is a prerequisite for a new world even in our time. In today's environment solid foundational truths are needed to counter the onslaught of decadence and decay that sits daily at our doorsteps. Tough challenges face us at every turn in the road. Whether it be senseless street violence, abuse of the poor, the ever present threat of global warfare, substance abuse, environmental racism, escalation of the aids epidemic, the proliferation of babies birthing babies, same-sex marriage, misguided sexualized lyrics by well paid singers that would make our foreparents shiver in their graves, it is time for serious discourse on tough issues. Societal challenges not only face us at every turn, similar, yet tough issues face us within the Community of Faith. *Righteousness exalteth a nation but sin is a reproach to any people. (Proverbs 14: 34)*

For Reflection and Dialogue

1. Why are interpersonal relationships important for ministry in today's church?

2. Should a church's ministry be dominated by any gender?

3. Discuss ways can effect total involvement of members in the ministries of the church.

4. Discuss the meaning of unity in unleashing the church's potential.

EPILOGUE

Kingdom Hope and Possibilities for the City

Exodus 3:21 [God to Moses] *"When ye go, ye shall not go empty."*

In various ways I have sought to point to the causes of the misery, alienation and suffering in our inner cities. The challenge that face each of us is how may we link our faith with justice? How ought we to combine the pastoral and the prophetic if we are to reclaim the city by seeking the "welfare of the city." Jeremiah's counsel to Israel, a pilgrim people in exile, was to "seek the welfare of the city where I have sent you into exile and pray to the Lord on its behalf." My task is to challenge the perspective we bring to inner city ministry. This means re-thinking our identity, our approach and our theology for the city.

Perspective is crucial. My perspective is an announcement of where I stand in history. It informs others of my locus in the world. My journey informs my perspective, likewise my perspective informs my journey. My perspective has been impacted by my heritage and culture. My method of thinking, the way I approach particular circumstances had already been conditioned and informed by the cultural presuppositions that are a part of my past history. My self-identity was formed and shaped out of a particular socio-historical context. Identity informs my future.

My thought pattern is shaped by cultural presuppositions derived from my past

My perspective was decisively impacted long before my early education began. It began taking shape as an African-American growing upon Florida's East Coast. Pompano Beach Florida, during the 1950's and 1960's, was far removed from being an Urban icon. In fact it was just the reverse, a small farm town community nestled halfway between Miami and West Palm Beach and next to Fort Lauderdale. We were constantly and yet painfully reminded of our place in this small segregated southern town.

As in many Southern towns during that period, the railroad track was the dividing line between two separate and unequal societies one Euro-American and one African-American with well defined boundaries characterized by classism and racism. Our parents often reminded us to say "yes sir" and "no sir" to all Euro-Americans regardless to age. We were to step off the curb if need be in order to allow Euro-Americans to pass. We were conditioned to make-believe that we were going along in order to get along. My perspective was being shaped.

With the press for integration after the passage of the Civil Rights Bill, Southern states constructed the finest schools possible to maintain a separate but equal facade. While the physical facilities were equal, we received second-rate books from the white high school across town with no apologies. The only thing that helped us survive was committed African-American teachers under a committed African-American principal, the late Mrs. Blanche G. Ely, a distinguished educator and mentor. Principal Ely fought many battles with the power structure and abhorred the idea of working on farms during class time. To this day it remains a mystery as to why the Euro-American football team consisting of persons who never saw a bean farm were called the bean-pickers, while the African-American team was called the tigers. Racism often operates by a strange logic. My perspective was being formed and my identity was being shaped.

Added to this was the presentation of a blonde, blue-eyed Europeanized Christ, the product of an artist's imagination. But once we discovered the manly virile Christ of Scripture, we became distrustful and uncomfortable with a Euro-centric Christ that did not square with our manhood. We longed for a Christ who would break the bonds of oppression and set the captives free. We longed for a God who would keep His word, even if the heavens passed away. We needed a God who was bound to His people by covenant. A covenant is a treaty, an agreement, a political instrument , it has such terms as "if you will be my people, I will be your God." We needed a political God. Should you enter the urban icon as a missioner, "do not go empty."

In the urban icon, the prophetic and the evangelistical must unite. Howard Snyder calls upon the church to be prophetically evangelistic and evangelistically prophetic. There must be a recounting of the old story in such a way that boneyards of despair are transformed into islands of hope. There must be prophetic protest against evils ensconced in social structures that war against the soul and prevent people from achieving wholeness and maximizing their potential.

As we approach the twenty first century change for the church is not optional. Churches who refuse to change will become ecclesiastical museums encased in Jurassic Park rhetoric. In reality we will not save the cities in our times, but we can make a difference. We must live on the cutting edge of where God is moving so future generations can attest to the fact that there lived a people who made a difference by etching their footprints in the sand. There lived a people whose hope was in their God and who did not come empty.

APPENDIX I

THE NEW LIFE CLASS

Series 1   Historical Background of Your Church and Its Emergence Significance of Ordinances

Series 2   Humankind as Sinner

Series 3   Eternal Life

Series 4   The Spirit Filled Life

Series 5   Stewardship

Series 6   Victorious Living

Series 7   Sharing Your Faith

Appendix

SERIES 2   HUMANKIND AS SINFUL

I   DEFINITION OF SIN- Derived from several root words; *awon*= iniquity, *Shagah*= err, *Pesha*= rebellion, *Wi* =wicked   Sin=state or condition of the soul where one violates God's law and lives in rebellion against God. Sin= is manifested as separation, alienation, rebellion, brokenness, failure to do something in relation to humankind or God

II   We can Sin either by Commission= committing certain acts as blasphemy, adultery, etc. or Omission= failure to do what one should do see James 4: 17; Sin is the precondition of evil; evil is the absence of good

III   Did you know that we were- Born in Sin? Psalm 51: 5 Did you know that all have sinned? See Romans 3: 23. We were created in the image of (likeness of God). The image of God (Imago Dei) is in every person. When Adam sinned in Eden (the Fall) the image in Adam=humankind was marred. Since the first sin of Adam and Eve the human race has inherited the consequences.

IV   There we cannot save ourselves- Ephesian 2: 8-9 God is merciful and does not want to punish us. God is just and therefore must punish sin. The problem is how can a gracious and loving God resolve such a dilemma?

Concluding Note
Next session we will explore the meaning of the greatest offer ever made by the greatest person who ever lived. In preparation read Romans 10:9, 1 John 3: 5, Titus 3: We are created in the image of God. The image is marred and defaced by sin. We discuss our need for grace. Eph. 3: 8 We would proceed to Series 3 on Eternal Life When God gives us the gift of eternal life through the free gift of salvation He also justifies and sanctifies us at the moment of the new birth.

SERIES 3   **THE GIFT OF ETERNAL LIFE**

Lesson Plan

I. WHAT IS THE NEW BIRTH?

Having been born in sin and shaped in iniquity we cannot save ourselves or merit our way to heaven by performing good deeds. Ephesian 2: 8-9 - "By grace are we saved through faith..." However SAVING FAITH is the key to the NEW BIRTH. Saving faith is trusting Jesus Christ alone for eternal life. The NEW BIRTH is an experience of transformation that takes place within the heart of a sinner who after repentance believes upon Christ alone for eternal life and thereby confesses it. Jesus said...*Verily, Verily I say unto you, he that believeth on me hath everlasting life.* John 6: 47 *"He that believeth...i.e. he that trusteth...he that resteth.* Not by works: not by intellectual and mental assent; one cannot think ones way to God- Romans 10: 9, Titus 3: 5 It is through the new birth that we received the assurance of eternal life. John 6: 47 Verily, verily I say unto you...   I John 4: 13 - Hereby we know that...I John 3: 14- We know that we have passed from death unto life...After you exercise saving faith in Jesus Christ satan will challenge you to whether or not you are saved. Remember God does not act on feelings (emotion), but faith alone. Doubt will come to the new believer, but remember the Holy Spirit has just wrought a miracle in you without doing anything except receiving it. He will seal your faith exercised from your heart. You are sealed unto the day of redemption.

II. REPENTANCE

True repentance precedes the new birth. Repentance is not merely crying; not merely feeling sorry for one's transgressions. Repentance is derived from the Greek term *"metanoia"* which means change of heart, mind and direction. When a person truly repents by faith they experience forgiveness of sins which prepares them for the free gift of salvation. God forgives us and relieves us of our sense of guilt. Guilt fractures the human personality, creates anxiety, depression and wreaks havoc in the human heart. Godly sorrow worketh repentance. Forgiveness means relationship restored. That is the meaning of divine forgiveness. That is the good news of the Gospel.

III WHAT HAPPENS TO OUR SINS?

According to Hebrews 9: 22 "Without the shedding of blood there is no remission of sins"
John 1: 29 "Behold the Lamb.." I John 1: 7- "And the blood of Jesus Christ His Son cleanseth..." Your sins?

They are FORGIVEN..................................Ephesians 4: 32
They are BlOTTED OUT...........................Isaiah 44:22
They are COVERED..................................Psalm 85: 2
They are REMOVED.................................Psalm 103: 12
They are CAST INTO THE SEA................Micah 7: 19
They are HID...Hosea 12: 12
They are HID BEHIND GOD'S BACK.....Isaiah 38: 17
They are FORGOTTEN..............................Isaiah 43: 25
CONCLUSION OF THE MATTER...........Isaiah 1: 18

IV JUSTIFICATION BY FAITH ALONE

To one who believes in Jesus Christ, God reckons or declares that person to be righteous. It is as though we were on death row and the executioner was about to invoke the instrument of death. Then comes Jesus and exchanges places with us and becomes what we are in order that we might become like Him. We are fully pardoned. Jesus alone drops all charges and declares case dismissed. We are not on parole earning our freedom, continuing to pay the debts for our crimes. He who knew no sin became sin that we might become the righteousness of God. He comes down to where we are so we can come up to where he is. We are justified by "saving faith." Faith is response to God in such a way that life is lived in a new way, always in response to God's revealed will. It is not fanciful or fantasy; it is trusting Jesus Christ alone for assurance for eternal life. Justification assures us of being made right in God's sight by faith in His promises. It gives us right standing before God. Justification brings us into a place of highest privilege where we confidently stand, live and joyfully look forward to actually becoming all that God has in mind for us to become.

V SANCTIFICATION

Literally sanctification means "the act of setting something apart"; act of consecration; to be separated in principle from sin to God through union with

Jesus Christ. Sanctification is two-fold. It is divine and human. In John 17: 19, Jesus sets Himself apart from Bethlehem's cradle to Calvary. I Thess. 5: 23 **The Divine Aspect** see: 1 Cor. 6: 11, 19-20, e.g. Jeremiah 1: 5 also Galatians 1: 15. The Human Aspect see 2 Chron. 29: 5, 2 Tim. 2: 21, 2 Cor. 6: 17. In 2 Cor. 7: 1 we are told to do things which we often beg God to do. We are admonished to literally "come out from among them and be separate and touch not the unclean thing."
What can be Sanctified?

Series 4   THE SPIRIT- FILLED LIFE

1. Why the Holy Spirit?

The primary purpose of the Holy Spirit is not "speaking in tongues" or a series of indescribable raptures, or to receive a special "Second Blessing" for one's personal enjoyment. According to Paul the Apostle "tongues" are for a sign not to those who believe but for those who believe not." Tongues should be viewed as one of the many significant consequences of the Baptism in the Holy Spirit rather than "initial evidence." In the book of Acts there are a few exceptions where tongues were not present at the inception of the Holy Spirit baptism. The experience of the Spirit Baptism is not an end in itself that would be selfishness), but rather a means to an end...pointing persons to Christ. It can be categorically stated that the purpose of the Spirit Baptism is to equip the Body of Christ for service, vocation and empowerment for the task of world evangelization. (See Acts 1: 8 and Acts 5: 42) The Holy Spirit is the third person in the Trinity. He has many names. E.g. Spirit of God; of Truth; of Adoption; of Christ; of Glory; of Grace; of Promise; of Wisdom.

11. Is the Baptism in the Holy Spirit Optional?

When you purchase an automobile you may be given the choice of adding optional equipment. But is this so with the Holy Spirit? The Spirit is to the divine life what blood is for human life. It is essential for activity, thought and personal relationships. See Luke 24:49 The Spirit Baptism does not make one holier, but it does make one more useful. The Baptism is not received as a definite work of grace but as a gift of God.   (See

Acts 11: 15 - 17) Believers in the Book of Acts were commanded to wait for the promise of the Father. The offices of the Holy Spirit are varied: Comforter; Teacher; Revealer; Giver; Justifier; Quickner; Searcher; Renewer, Paraclete.

Conclusion:

Many believers are not filled with the Holy Spirit because they are too full of self, prejudices, traditions, worldly ambitions, pride and preconceived ideas and many other things which hinder the infusion of the Spirit. In order to be filled you must first be emptied. There is no filling without an emptying. To be Spirit-filled means to be Spirit-controlled. (See Ephesians 5:18ff.) You must give full consent to being emptied of anything which stands between you and the Holy Spirit and allow God to do what you cannot do and be willing to receive what has been promised. The Holy Spirit is not an "it". He is a Person with intelligence and will. He comes in His fulness when enjoined by faith.

SERIES 5   ON STEWARDSHIP

1. **Stewardship** has to do with the sharing of the whole of our resources for the work of God's Kingdom in the earth. Jesus taught and believed that there is more joy and happiness in a life of giving than there is in a life of acquiring and having. From Jesus we learn the wisdom of trying to give ourselves a way. The scriptural model for the collection is found in 1 Corinthians 16: 1 -4. Stewardship in essence is management. We are encouraged to give systematically in and through the church as a way to bring honor and glory to God. In the Old Testament the presentation of unblemished animal sacrifices brought honor to God. In the New Testament the giving of the sacrifice of praise is encouraged for all believers. Giving orderly and systematic rather than spasmodic brings us under discipline.

11. **Time, Talent and Material Resources** embraces the core of our giving. We are admonished to give ourselves, time, talents, energy combined with encouragement and affirmation to those around us. Giving generously places us in a position to receive the blessings promised to the tither (see Malachi 3: 10 and Matthew 23: 23).

111. **Better to Give than to Receive**- Acts 20: 35 Generous giving increases our capacity to receive both the blessings of God and the favor of others- Luke 6: 38. It is the spirit in which we give that is decisive for our well being.

CONCLUSION: a solid theology of stewardship encourages the believer to give not merely to be blessed but rather because we are blessed. Such a theology prevents us from making God a "cosmic heavenly Bellhop" (E. Stanley Jones). Remember Jesus Christ was the Supreme Sacrifice. God does not promise us success and prosperity but He expects us to be faithful. We are encouraged to appear before the Lord with the sacrifice of praise and thanksgiving.

SERIES 6   VICTORIOUS LIVING

Lesson Plan

I. To encourage new believers to deliberately seek victorious living. This is the first lesson in Christian discipleship. New believers should grasp the two major defenses against Satan found in Ephesians 6: 10 - 12; Luke 4: 1, Matthew 26: 41. They should guard against three areas of temptation mention in I John 2: 16- Lust of the flesh, of the eyes and the pride of life.

II. According to Luke 6: 40 "A disciple...when he is fully taught will be like his teacher" (RSV) The goal for the new Christian is to become a Kingdom person. A Kingdom person is a disciple under the Lordship of Jesus Christ committed to developing and shaping one's character like Christ and willing to reproduce oneself in others according to the mandate of the Kingdom. A disciple is a follower, learner and servant of Jesus Christ and His Kingdom. The call of God implores all believers to participate with Him in the cosmic reconciliation of all things. Such a call is undergirded by obedience, discipline and a commitment to covenant.

III. As the vision of the Kingdom begins to crystallize, character formation takes shape. The formation of character in the new believer leads to maturity. This is the beginning of the quest toward victorious living in this world.

Appendix 151

SERIES 7 SHARING YOUR FAITH

Lesson Plan

I. **God's Primary Agenda-** The new believer is admonished to become a soul winner according to Daniel 12: 3. The example of Jesus encounter with the woman at the well of Samaria is a model for new believers to embrace. Since Christ has set you free you are to be a witness for the Lord.

II. See Like 19: 10 as a model Scripture in following our Lord in the work of redemption. Christ seeks the lost, the bruised and broken and creates a people unto himself. E. Stanley Jones once said "if we are not reconcilers it may be that we have never been reconciled." Sharing one's faith can be a source of encouragement for new believers. New believers should be encouraged to seek a passion for souls. The Holy Spirit will give to those who ask.

New believers should be admonished to first seek to lead their family and then friends to Jesus Christ. According to Jesus the field is the world.

Conclusion: Read Dr. D. James Kennedy's book *Evangelism Explosion* as a hands on guide for evangelism and outreach.

Appendix II

FOURTEEN WAYS TO KILL A CHURCH

1. Don't come

2. If you come, come late.

3. When you come, come with a grouch.

4. At every service ask yourself, "what am I getting out of this ?"

5. Never accept a position. It is much better to stay outside and criticize.

6. Visit other churches about half the time to let your minister know you are not tied to him. After all there is nothing like independence.

7. Let the pastor earn his money by doing all the work.

8. Sit back and never sing. Should you sing, please sing out of tune and behind everyone else.

9. Never pay in advance. Wait until you get your money's worth, and then wait longer.

10. Never encourage the minister. If you enjoyed a sermon, remain silent. After all many preachers have been ruined by flattery

Appendix

11. It is good to tell your pastors failings and shortcomings to strangers. They might be a long time finding them out.

12. Of course you can't be expected to get new members for the church with such a pastor.

13. If your church happens to be harmonious, call it apathy or indifference or lack of zeal or anything under the sun except what it is.

14. If there happens to be a few zealous workers in the church, make a tremendous protest in the church, against the church being run by a clique.

Robert Freeman- Ministers Manual

Appendix III

PHILOSOPHY OF MINISTRY
(From 25 years of pastoral experience)

- Treat all persons and especially members with respect
- Never violate the confidence of those you counsel
- God rewards faithfulness
- It is possible to exert influence without being impressive
- Cultivate a friendly church and the dividends will surprise you.
- Avoid "fussing" at your people from the pulpit.
- Specialize in developing people rather than programs
- Make sure you are relevant without being right at all costs.
- It is difficult to row and rock the boat at the same time
- A ministry-driven and Christ-centered church will be fruitful.
- Respect differences in people without violating their personhood.
- Never betray private confidences with board members in a public setting.
- Every person is peculiarly endowed with uniqueness. Appreciate the facts that their gifts have been shaped by God for His purpose.
- Always be open to constructive criticism, it can enable you to grow.
- Avoid siding with specific groups or cliques in your church so you can be prophetic as you minister to God's people.
- Keep in mind people are more important than property
- Never wait for the perfect time to do what you deem to be important. People who wait for perfect conditions never get anything significant done.
- Love is more that a tingling feeling. It is action and caring deeds.

- A church that loves will grow.
- Live in honesty with the consciousness that we live in a moral universe.
- Try growing with your people. Cultivate confidence and win their trust.
- Be intentional about doing the right thing without worrying about doing everything right.
- Avoid people with a "Lilliputian" mentality that holds on to small trivial things. In a matter of time they will sink major ships.
- Commitment is more important that membership.
- Never view money spent on evangelism outreach as an expense, it is an investment.
- "Kingdom work, done God's way, will never lack God's support."

"The wilderness and the solitary place shall be glad for them; and the desert shall rejoice, and blossom as the rose ; It shall blossom abundantly, and rejoice even with joy and singing."

Isaiah 35: 2   KJV

Source Notes

Chapter 1

1. There is no substitute for the pastoral experience. It alone gives credence to what one has learned in seminary. Every seminary professor should be required to engage in pastoral ministry as a prerequisite for teaching.

2. My initial thinking about the need to develop Kingdom people rather than church people was radically challenged by Howard A. Snyder's *Liberating the Church: The Ecology of Church and Kingdom* his *A Kingdom Manifesto*

3. This definition of prayer came from the late United Methodist preacher and missionary to India for more than fifty years, E. Stanley Jones. See his classic devotional, *The Way*, Garden City, N.Y.: Doubleday, 1978. My thinking about prayer and the devotional life has never been the same since encountering the writings of this saintly personality. I suggest that one should be intentional about reading everything he has written.

4. See Ronald J. Sider, *One-Sided Christianity?*, Grand Rapids Michigan: Zondervan Publishing House, 1993, p. 62

5. Charles Swindoll, President of Dallas Theological Seminary pastored in Southern California a few miles from my last pastorate. His commentary on attitude is unusually profound. See his *Strengthening Your Grip*, Dallas, London, Vancouver, 1982, p. 207. I have valued his insights over a period of time in certain aspects of his thoughts.

6. See Lloyd Perry's *Getting the Church on Target*, Chicago: Moody Press, 1977, p. 7

Chapter 2

1. See article by Dr. Bong Rin Ro, "Producing a Growing Church" in Mission Today 95, Part 2, Berry Publishing Services, Evanston, Il.

2. George G. Hunter III, "Helping the Small Church Grow" in Church Growth Strategies that Work, (ed.) Lyle E. Schaller, Nashville: A Abingdon, 1980

Source Notes

3. Steven Wineman, *The Politics of Human Services*, Boston: South End Press, 1984, p. 124

4. Evelyn Underhill, *The Spiritual Life*, New York: harper and Row, n.d., p. 61

5. Henri J.M. Nouwen, *With Open Hands*, Notre Dame : Ave Maria Press, 1972, p. 94 This classic devotional is a must reading for anyone interested in expanding their understanding of the prayer life.

Chapter 3

1. Samuel D. Proctor, "The Theological Validation of Black Worship" in *The Black Christian Worship Experience* (ed) M.W. Costen & D.L. Swann, Black Church Scholars Series, Volume IV, 1992

2. See *Cut Loose Your Stammering Tongue*, (ed.) Dwight N. Hopkins & George C.L. Cummings, Orbis Books, N.Y., 1991, p. 7

3. Kenneth Leech, *Experiencing God: Theology as Spirituality*, Harper, San Francisco, 1985, p. 162

4. Proctor, *Ibid.*, 222

5. Bob Sorge, *Exploring Worship* (privately published, 1987, Canandaqua, N.Y., p.40

6. James White, *Protestant Worship*, Louisville: Westminster/John Knox Press, 1989

7. See *Time,* Fall, 1992 vol. 140 no 27, Special Issue, "Beyond the Year 2000, What to Expect in the New Millennium"

8. Avery Dulles, *Models of the Church*, N.Y.: Image Books, 1978, p. 21

9. *Ibid.,* p. 29

Source Notes

10. T.S. Kuhn, *The Structure of Scientific Revolutions*, 2nd ed.,, Chicago: University of Chicago Press, 1970, p. 175

11. Dulles, *Loc. Cit.*, p. 31

Chapter 4

1. Master is defined as one in control or authority; a person of consummate skill in an art, technique. See *The New Webster Dictionary*, N. Y.: Lexicon Publications, 1990

2. Howard A. Snyder, *A Kingdom Manifesto*, Downers Grove, Ill: Intervarsity Press, 1985

3. Richard F. Lovelace, "Thy Kingdom Come on Earth and in Heaven" *Colloquy on the Hallowing of Life*, Indiana: Notre Dame, 1982, p. 2

4. John Bright, *The Kingdom of God*, Nashville: Abingdon Press, 1953, p.7

5. E. Stanley Jones, *Is the Kingdom of God Realism?*, N.Y. Abingdon-Cokesbury, 1940, p. 53

6. Howard A. Snyder, Liberating the Church, Downers Grove, Ill., Intervarsity Press, 1983, p. 10

7. Adapted from *Collier's Encyclopedia*, Volume 10, 1990

8. See Steve Sjogren, "Servant Hearts, the key to Effective Evangelism," in *Ministries Today*, July/August 1993, Volume II, November 4

10. This thesis is developed in Sjogren'e recent book *Conspiracy of Kindness,* Ann Arbor, Michigan: Vine Books, 1993; Also see George G. Hunter III, How to reach Secular People, Nashville: Abingdon, 1992

Source Notes

Chapter 5

1. Matthew Levy, "Building the Empire City" in *The Sciences*, Dec. 1980, New York Academy of Sciences

2. From Viv Grigg " 1000 by 2000" in *City Watch*, volume 6, no. 4, 1991, a bi-monthly publication of the Institute of Global Urban Studies, Pasadena California

3. Thomas Toch, "The Schools an Agenda for Change" *U.S. News & World Report*. October 5, 1992

4. Leonard Lovett, "Kingdom Living, Racism and Reconciliation." *Charisma,* April 1993, Volume 18, no. 9., p. 14

5. David Claerbaut, *Urban Ministry*, Grand Rapids, Michigan: Zondervan, 1983, p. 130

6. Joseph Bardnt, *Liberating Our White Ghetto*, Minneapolis, Augsburg Press

7. George W. Webber, *Today's Church, A Community of Exiles and Pilgrims,* Nashville: Abingdon, 1979, p. 63

8. My first serious mentor in social ethics was the late Dr. Kenneth Smith, Crozer Theological Seminary Professor. I was introduced at an early stage in my theological pilgrimage to the relationship between theology and politics. For the Christian there is no neutral ground when it comes to the arena of politics. There is no dualism between the sacred and the secular since all comes under the governance of God. We are reminded in the sacred writ that there were "saints in Caesar's household."

9. E. Stanley Jones, *Is the Kingdom of God Realism?* N.Y.: Abingdon Cokesbury, 1940, p. 59 - 60

10. Robert W. Pazmino, *Principles and Practices of Christian Education*, Grand Rapids, Michigan, Baker, 1992, p. 46, 51

Source Notes

11. I discussed the primacy of love over faith in the New Testament in my article "Positive Confession Theology" in the *Dictionary of the Pentecostal Charismatic Movement*, Grand Rapids Michigan :Zondervan, 1988

Chapter 6

1. Lyle E. Schaller, *Assimilating New Members*, Nashville: Abingdon, 1978, p. 23

2. See Chuck Ashman, *The Gospel According to Billy*. Lyle Stuart Inc.: Secaucus, N. J., 1977

Chapter 7

See Washington Post, Monday, December 9, 1996

Chapter 8

1. See my *Opening the Front Door of Your Church*, Lanham, Md.: Pneuma Life, 1994, p. 44

2. Robert E. Webber, *Worship is a Verb*, Abbott Martyn, Nashville, Tn., 1992, p. 7

3. Dean M. Kelley, *Why Conservative Churches are Growing*, N.Y.: Harper & Row, 1972, p. 162

4. Gary Collins, *Christian Counseling: A Comprehensive Guide*, Waco: Word, 1980, p. 23

5. Collins, *Ibid.*, p. 24

6. Collins, *Loc. Cit*

7. Merton P Strommen, *Five Cries of Youth*, N. Y. Harper, 1974

8 Jewelle Taylor Gibbs,(ed) *Young, Black and Male in America: An Endangered Species*, N.Y..: Auburn House, 1988, 1 ff

9. For more recent reliable statistical data on Black males see Bobby William Austin (ed.) *Repairing the Breach: Report on the National Task Force on African American Men and Boys*, Dillon: Alpine Guild, Inc, 1996, p. 22 ff.

10. See George Barna's *Baby Busters: The Disillusioned Generation*, Chicago: Northfield Publishing Co., 1994 and *Reaching Generation X*

11. See Karen Ritchie, *Marketing to Generation X*, N.Y. Lexington Books, 1995

12. From "Black Like Who? Rap, Respect and the New Generation Gap" *Newsweek*, May 17, 1997

13. Wayne C. Barrett, *Clergy Personal Finance*, Nashville: Abingdon, 1990, p. 9

Chapter 9

1. Georgia Harkness, *Understanding the Christian Faith*, Nashville: Abingdon Press, 1992 [1947], p. 156

2. Gary W. Kuhne, *The Dynamics of Discipleship Training*, Grand Rapids, Michigan" Zondervan, 1978, p. 34

3. Don Hawkins, *Master Discipleship*, Grand Rapids, Michigan: Kregel resources, 1996, p. 9

4. Waylon B. Moore, *Multiplying Disciples*, The New Testament Method for Church Growth, Colorado Springs: NavPress, 1981

5. Juan Carlos Ortiz, *Call to Discipleship*, Plainfield, New Jersey: **Logos, 1975**

6. E. Stanley Jones, *The Way*. Garden City. N.Y.: Doubleday Galilee Book, 1978, p 215

Notes

Source Notes

7. Gerald L. Dahl, *Why Christian Marriages are Breaking Up*, Nashville, N.Y: Thomas Nelson Publishers, 1979, p. 78

8. Tony Allesandra and Phil Hunsaker, *Communicating at Work*, N.Y. Fireside Book by Simon and Schuster, 1993, p. 121ff

9. H.Wayland Cummings &Charles Somervill,*Overcoming Communication Barriers* in the Church, Valley Forge: Judson Press, 1981, p. 158

10. Cummings and Somervill, *Op. Cit.*, p. 82

11 Allensadra & Hunsaker, *Op. Cit.*, p. 98

Chapter 10

1. Paul K. Hatt & Albert J. Reiss, Jr., (ed) *Cities and Societies*, N.Y. The Free Press of Glencoe Inc, 1961, p. 20

2. Ellen M Trimmer, *Building Interpersonal Relationships*, Chicago Moody Press, 1972, P. 11 ff

3. Hatt & Reiss. *Ibid.*, P. 477

4. Elizabeth O'Connor, *Call to Commitment*, Harper & Row Publishers, N.Y.: 1963, 114 ff

5. Jewelle Taylor Gibbs, *Op. Cit.*, p. Xxiii

6. Elmer Towns, *America's Fastest Growing Churches*, Nashville: Impact Books, 1972

Suggested Resources for Ministry in an Urban Setting

Adams, Jay E., *Handbook of Church Discipline*, Zondervan 1986.
Agnew, John Mercer, and David Sopher, eds. *The City in Cultural Context*. Boston: Allen and Unwin, 1984.
Barndt, Joseph, *Dismantling Racism*. Minn: Augsburg, 1991.
Bakke, Raymond J., *The Urban Christian*. Downers Grove, IL.: InterVarsity, 1987.
Banfield, Edward C., *Political Influence*. N.Y.: Free Press, 1961.
Bourne, Larry S. (Ed.), *Internal Structure of the City*. N.Y.: London:Oxford University, 1971.
Barna, George, *Marketing the Church*, Nav Press, 1986,
Callahan, Edward, *Twelve Keys to an Effective Church*, Harper & Row, 1983.
Callow, Alexander B. Jr., ed. *American Urban History*. Oxford: Oxford University Press, 1982.
Chewning, Richard C., (Ed.), *Biblical Principles and Public Policy*. Colorado Springs, Colo: NavPress, 1991.
Claerbaut, David. *Urban Ministry*. Grand Rapids, MI: Zondervan, 1983.
Conn, Harvey. *A Clarified Vision for Urban Ministry*. Ministry Resources Library, 1987.
Clark, Kenneth B., *Dark Ghetto: Dilemmas of Social Power*. N.Y.:
Chaney, Charles, *Church Planting at the End of the Twentieth Century*, Tyndale House, 1986.
Costas, Orlando *The Church and Its Mission: A Shattering Critique From the Third World*, Tyndale, 1974.
Dulles, Avery, *Models of the Church*, Image, 1978.
Dawson, John. *Taking the Cities for God*. Lake Mary FL: Creation House, 1989.
Dayton, Edward R. and Samuel Wilson, eds. *Unreached Peoples* . Elgin, IL: David C. Cook, 1992.
ˮn, Craig, ed. *The Urban Mission*. Grand Rapids, MI.: Eerdmans, ˮ974.
ˮ, & Maynard E.S., *Healing for The City*. Grand Rapids, MI.: ˮvan, 1991.
ˮ *Cities on a Hill*. N.Y.: Simon and Schuster, 1986.
ˮ *In Deed*, Eerdmans, 1975.

Bibliography

Gillion, Arthur B. & Eisner, Simon, *The Urban Pattern*. N.Y. D. Van Nostrand Co., 1980.

Greenway, Roger. *Apostles to the City*. Grand Rapids, MI:; 1979.

_____, editor. *Discipling the City.* Grand Rapids: Baker Book House, 1979.

Greenway, Roger S. and Timothy M. Monsma. *Cities: Mission's New Frontier*. Grand Rapids, MI: Baker book House, 1989.

Gulick, John. *The Humanity of Cities: An Introduction to Urban Societies*. Granley, MA: Bergin and Garvey, 1989.

Hannerz, Ulf. *Exploring the City: Inquiries Toward Urban Anthropology*. Columbia Univ. Press, 1980.

Harre, Alan F., *Close the Back Door, Ways to Create A Caring Congregation* Fellowship, Concordia, 1984.

Hyles, Jack, *Let's Build an Evangelistic Church*, Sword of the Lord Publishers, 1962.

Hess, M. J. and Bartlett, L., *How to Have A Giving Church*, Abingdon, 1974.

Hesselgrave, David, *Planting Churches Cross-Culturally*, Baker, 1980.

Kendall, R. T., *Tithing A Call to Serious Biblical Giving*, Lamplighter, 1982.

Jones, James M., *Prejudice and Racism*. Reading, Mass: Addison-Wesley Pub. Co., 1972.

Jones, E. Stanley. *The Reconstruction of the Church* -

Kelley, Dean M., *Why Conservative Churches Are Growing*, Harper & Row, 1972.

Kelley, Allen and Jeffrey G. Williamson. *What Drives Third World Cities Growth?* Princeton, NJ: Princeton University Press, 1977.

Kinloch, Graham C., *The Sociology of Minority Group Relations*. Englewood Cliffs, N.J.: Prentice Hall, 1979.

Kochman, Thomas, *Black and White Styles In Conflict*. Chicago: Univ. of Chicago Press, 1981.

Kozol, Jonathan. *Rachel and Her Children: Homeless Families in America*. N.Y.: Crown, 1988.

_____ *Savage Inequalities*, N.Y., Harper Perennial, 1992

Kyle, John E., *Urban Mission*. Downers Grove, ILL: Intervarsity Press, 1988.

Jones, E. Stanley, *Mastery, The Art of Mastering Life*, A

_____ *The Way*
_____ *Abundant Living*
_____ *Christian Maturity*
_____ *Conversion*
_____ *The Divine Yes*
_____ *Is the Kingdom of God Realism?*

Ladd, George E., *The Gospel of the Kingdom*, Eerdmans, 1959.

LaPierre, Dominique. *The City of Joy*. New York, N.Y.: Warner Books, 1985.

Lee, Robert. *The Church and The Exploding Metropolis*, Richmond VA: John Knox Press, 1965.

Linthicum, Robert. *City of God: City of Satan*. Grand Rapids: Zondervans, 1991.

_____. *Empowering the Poor*. Monrovia: MARC, 1991.

Meeks, Wayne A. *The First Urban Christians: The Social World of the Apostle Paul.* New Haven, CN: Yale, 1983.

Miller, Randall M. and Thomas D. Marzik, eds. *Immigrants and Religion in Urban America.* Philadelphia: Temple University Press, 1977.

Molnar, Thomas, *Twin Powers: Politics and the Sacred*. Grand Rapids MI: Eerdmans, 1988.

Newbigin, Leslie, *The Gospel In a Pluralist Society.* Grand Rapids, MI: Eerdmans, 1989.

Miller, Herb, *How to Build A Magnetic Church*, Abingdon, Abingdon, 1987.

McGavran, D. and Hunter, E.E., *Church Growth Strategies That Work*, Abingdon, 1980.

_____ *Understanding Church Growth*, Eerdmans 1980.

Martin, E., McIntosh, G. *Finding Them Keeping Them*; Broadman, 1992.

Moberg, D.O., *The Great Reversal*, Holman, 1977.

Pasquariello, Ronald, Donald W. Shriver, Jr., and Alan Geyer. *Redeeming the City*.New York: Pilgrim Press, 1982.

P   E.H., *Working the Angles*, Eerdmans, 1987.

           A. and Perry, L.M., *Churches In Crisis*, Moody, 1981.

                Strubhar, J. R., *Evangelistic Preaching*, Moody 1979.

                Getting the Church on Target, Moody, 1977.

                an Church Education. Birmingham, AL: Religious

Bibliography

Rose, Arnold M. *The Power Structure*. N.Y.: Galazy Book, 1967.
Snyder, Howard A., *Liberating the Church*, Intervarsity Press, 1983.
    _____ *A Kingdom Manifesto*, (IVP)
    _____ *The Problems of Wineskins* (IVP)
    _____ *The Community of the King* (IVP)
    _____ *Models of the Kingdom*, Abingdon, 1991
Snyder, T. Richard, *Once You Were No People*, Meyer Stone Book, 1988.
    _____ *Divided We Fall*, Westminster/John Knox Press, 1992.
Schaller, Lyle E., *Hey, That's Our Church*, Abingdon, 1975.
    _____ *Impact of the Future*, Abingdon
    _____ *Parish Planning*, Abingdon
    _____ *Survival Tactics In the Parish*, Abingdon
    _____ *The Change Agent*, Abingdon
    _____ *Effective Church Planning*, Abingdon
Shelly, Bruce L., *The Gospel and the American Dream*, Multnomah, 1989.
Spurgeon, Charles H., *The Soul Winner*, Eerdmans, 1963.
Shockley, Donald G., *Free White and Christian*. Nashville: Abingdon, 1975.
Shriver, Donald W., and Ostrom, Karl A., *Is There Hope for The City?* Phila: Westminster Press, 1977.
Trujillo, Bishop Alfonso L., *Liberation or Revolution*, Our Sunday Visitor Inc., 1977.
Tonna, Benjamin. *Gospel for the Cities: A Socio-Theology of Urban Ministry*. Maryknoll: Orbis Books, 1982.
Terry, Robert W., *For Whites Only.* Grand Rapids, MI: Eerdmans, 1975.
Vesperi, Maria D. *City of Green Benches: Growing Old in a New Downtown*. Ithaca, NY: Cornell University Press, 1985.
Vigil, James Diego. *Barrio Gangs Street Life and Identity in Southern California.* Austin: University of Texas Press, 1988.
Wallis, Jim, *Revive Us Again*, Abingdon, 1983.
Webber, George W., *Today's Church, A Community of Exiles and Pilgrims*, Abingdon, 1979.
    _____ *,God's Colony In Man's World*
Word Books Publisher, *Fresh Ideas For Preaching Worship and Evangelism,* 1982.
White, J., Blue, K., *Healing the Wounded*, Intervarsity Press, 1985.Weiss, Michael J. *The Clustering of America*. New York, NY: Harper and Row, 1988.

Whyte, William H., City: ***Rediscovering the Center***. Garden City, NJ: Doubleday, 1989.

Yon, William A. (ed)., ***Studies of Urban Churches:*** "To Build the City...Too Long a Dream." Washington, D.C.: The Alban Institute, 1989.

Ziegenhals, Walter E., ***Urban Churches in Transition***. New York, NY: Ilgram Press, 1978.